WILD ABOUT Notting Hill & NORTH KENSINGTON

CARNIVAL, MARKETS & GARDENS

By Andrew Wilson & Caroline MacMillan

Sponsored by

Winkworth

I would like to dedicate this book to to my wonderful children, Sam and Amy, and to my lovely wife Diana. – Andrew Wilson

Clockwise from top left: Ladbroke Square Garden, St John's Church, Portobello Road and the Grand Union Canal.

Contents

Welcome to Wild About Notting Hill & North Kensington	4
Notting Hill & North Kensington – A Short History of the Area	8
Ladbroke Square Garden	12
Kensington Park Road	24
Elgin Crescent	28
Arundel & Elgin Gardens	31
St John's Church	38
A walk around west Notting Hill	42
Arundel & Ladbroke Gardens	46
Lansdowne Crescent	54
Lansdowne Road	56
Westbourne Grove	58
Lansdowne & Clarendon Garden	67
Portobello Market	74
Notting Hill Carnival	80
Pembridge Square	86
Colville Mews	90
Colville Square	92
All Saints Road	94
St James's Gardens	98
Holland Park Avenue	104
Royal Crescent Garden	110
Norland Square	116
A walk around east Notting Hill	120
Wesley Square	124
Lancaster Green	126
Frestonia	130
Avondale Park	134
North Kensington	140
St Charles Hospital	142
Little Wormwood Scrubs	148
A walk around North Kensington	154
Ladbroke Grove	158
Acklam Road	160
Under the Westway	164
Kensal Road	170
Portobello Road	174
Bassett Road	178
Chesterton Road	180
Oxford and Cambridge Gardens	182
Kensington Memorial Park	186
Trellick Tower	190
Goldborne Road	192
Grand Union Canal	196

Welcome to Wild About Notting Hill & North Kensington

Welcome to the 12th book in my ever expanding series of books on the villages and towns of south and west London. Until the summer of 2015 I didn't really know the Notting Hill area that well. I was asked by a client to take some pictures and discovered to my delight that once off the beaten track, there was much to see. It was then that I shared my discovery with my historian and within minutes she had me thinking that this should be our next project. Her husband was born here, you see, and within days of half suggesting that I might do it, she was bombarding me with notes on the history of this and the photo opportunity of that. Astonishingly, she even produced a spreadsheet containing an alphabetical list of every street in the area, all of which she had recently walked and advising me of either a historical fact or a chance of a photograph. There was no chance I could back out now and I am so pleased that I didn't. From the beautiful hidden gardens and distinctive architecture to the colourful streets and bustling markets, I have loved my time cataloguing Notting Hill and North Kensington and I hope you enjoy what I discovered.

My books take well over a year to produce and with all my books, there are many people along the way who have helped me and none more so than my historian, Caroline MacMillan. This is our fourth book together and her energy is quite infectious and I look forward to our next 'campaign'. Besides being a historian, Caroline is also a local guide and as with our previous projects together, we have included within the book three brand new walks, where we literally wanted to take you from the page out onto the actual streets to discover for yourself what a wonderful place this is. Then there are my sponsors, Winkworth, who came to my aid in the summer, when my original backers got cold feet after Brexit. Alex from their Notting Hill office, took a chance with me and I am so pleased that he did. He and Sohail from their North Kensington office are rightly proud of their piece of London and I am very grateful to them both. Notting Hill is known for its gardens and from the outset I felt I needed to make something of this and I am very grateful to the six gardens that allowed me exclusive access to photograph the changing seasons in each. As well as the gardens, there are many other places featured in the book and wherever possible I have tried to thank as many of the people I have met along the way within the text. This year I was lucky enough to be joined by my daughter, Amy, for a few weeks in the summer as my 'intern' and it was really great to give her an inside view of what I get up too. Finally, I would like to thank my designer, Tim Ball, from Ball Design & Branding, who takes my pictures and makes them come alive on the page. I love photography and I pinch myself every warm and sunny day that I am out and about with my camera that I'm actually working. Many people say to me that the sun is always shining in my books and I hope that you experience some of this warmth too.

Andrew Wilson, October 2016

Josie, my constant companion, up on Little Wormwood Scrubs

Notting Hill & North Kensington

A SHORT HISTORY OF THE AREA
by Caroline MacMillan

As the 94 bus heads down the steep hill from Notting Hill Gate towards Shepherd's Bush, it is following the same route carved by Roman soldiers as they marched westwards from Londinium through the tree lined slopes lying north of the gently flowing Thames. After their departure the area attracted Saxon invaders and one family, the Cnottingas or 'Sons of Cnotta', established themselves in a clearing of the wooded area which was teaming with deer and wild boar. By 1066 this colony had disappeared and the surrounding land, part of Chenesitun, now known to us as Kensington, was given by William the Conqueror to Geoffrey, Bishop of Coutances with the prominent Norman de Vere family as the main tenant. Chenesitun was subsequently divided into three Manors, the most northern one encompassing the area where the Cnottingas had settled. By 1462 this manor house and its dependences was referred to as Knottyngesbernes, some twenty years later Notingbarons and in 1544 Nutingbars whilst the steep hill was known as Knottynghull. The dissolution of the monasteries by Henry VIII brought the manor lands under Crown control and his daughter, Elizabeth I, granted Knotting Barns to her Secretary of State, William Cecil, Baron of Burghley with royal ownership ending when the land was sold at the turn of the 17th century for £3,400 to a City of London Alderman, Sir Henry Anderson.

Whilst the Notting Hill of today is a bustling urban area, in the 18th century it was a small country hamlet either side of the main road to Uxbridge. As well as acting as a magnet to highwaymen attracted a large number of inns most of which have either disappeared completely such as the Coach and Horses, which was demolished to make way for the multi-storey Campden Hill Towers or, like the Old Swan, been incorporated into a modern development. During the seventeenth century extensive pits to extract gravel were dug either side of the road from Bayswater to Notting Hill

Below: Westbourne Grove taken around the turn of the last century (left) and today (right).

and when the Kensington Gravel Pits toll gate was erected by a Turnpike Trust at the junction where today's Pembridge Road meets the high street this led to that part of Notting Hill getting it's Gate. There were also some substantial residences, Stormont House built in 1786 now lies under Clanricarde Gardens and Norland House was located further down the hill but is remembered by the square of that name.

The woodlands of the northern part of Kensington gradually gave way to pastures and hayfields and a map of 1833 shows two major farms in the area, Notting Barns and Porto Bello. To the south west in Notting Dale the malleable yellow clay resulted in many acres turning into brickfields, the deep digging often creating large lakes, one which earned the nickname 'The Ocean' and was located where children now play in Avondale Park. The kiln standing in Walmer Road is a reminder of the Kensington Potteries established in the 1780s which produced tiles, drain pipes and pots for many years. This area was also known as The Piggeries after Samuel Lake, a chimney sweep who kept a few pigs, invited pig-keepers turned out of their smallholdings in what is now the Connaught Square area of Paddington to join him. By 1850 it was estimated there were more than 3,000 pigs and 1,000 residents living in squalid conditions in an area of eight acres. These were then joined by Romany gypsies with their horse drawn vans who duly established a permanent shanty town.

James Weller Ladbroke, owner of the Ladbroke Estate must have been relieved when entrepreneur John Whyte leased 140 acres of the slopes of Notting Hill and erected a seven foot wooden paling around them to enclose his Hippodrome racecourse. Although the top of the hill where St. John's church now stands offered splendid views of the first race in 1837, west London's answer to Ascot

Top: A 19th century drawing of the proposed church for St James's Gardens.

Bottom: The same scene today. Thank you to Irene, who lives in the Harrison Housing building at the eastern end of the square and who kindly invited me into her apartment to take this picture.

Thank you to Kensington Central Library, Phillimore Walk, for the old pictures used throughout this book.

was not a financial success as the heavy clay soil proved unsuitable for racing and the enterprise closed just four years later. But by now the area was looking attractive to property developers, the first stone of St James's Gardens was laid on 1st November 1847, between 1840 and 1870 grand houses rose round leafy crescents and squares on the Ladbroke Estate whilst at the top of the hill yet more elegant houses covered land around Chepstow Villas and Pembridge Square. The arrival of the Hammersmith and City Railway in 1864 encouraged development to the northern area and by 1880 the farm lands of the St. Quintin and Portobello estates had given way to bricks and mortar.

The first churches to be built were St. John's in 1845 standing on the crest of Ladbroke hill and Vulliamy's elegant

St. James Norland. All Saints in Talbot Road was designed in flamboyant Victorian Gothic style but due to financial problems the envisaged grand spire was never built and it had to wait several years for its interior decoration and furniture, in the meantime its derelict state earned it the nickname 'All Sinners in the Mud'. The Catholic church dedicated to St. Francis opened its doors in 1860 for worshippers living in the Dale whilst Nonconformists built the impressive twin-towered Horbury Chapel at the Gate, now the Kensington Temple. The rural countryside also attracted several religious orders, the closed order of Carmelite nuns still live peacefully in their 1878 St. Charles Square monastery but Dominican nuns eventually left their convent in Portobello Road which is now occupied by the Spanish School.

Private schools were available to those who could pay, others turned to the Church or Ragged Schools set up by generous benefactors. Norland House eventually became a Military Academy 'for the civil or military education of sons of the gentry', whilst the small kindergarten opened in 1876 by Miss Emily Lord in Norland Place, now part of Holland Park Avenue, continues there as a school for young children. As a result of the 1870 Education Act and the rapid expansion of the area's population the need for state schools became urgent so Buckingham Terrace School, since renamed Colville Primary, was built in 1879 and a year later the first pupils were taught at Sirdar Road L.C.C. School, now Avondale Park Primary.

With the proximity of good transport links by canal, road and rail, industry took over the remaining open spaces of North Kensington and in 1903 the Earl of Shrewsbury built his Clement-Talbot automobile factory whose impressive office frontage still overlooks Barlby Road. By the end of the First World War the only green spaces not covered with housing were Little Wormwood Scrubs and St. Quintin Park, the latter hosting the annual Notting Hill Flower and Home Improvement Show until the end of the 1920s when houses finally covered the area. The face of Notting Dale was changing again and though the piggeries and potteries had been cleared some of the replacement Victorian terraces became overcrowded and dilapidated and by the 1950s the council was replacing these with flats such as Henry Dickens Court and Lancaster West Estate, whilst the Olivia Hill housing association took over the

Left: Oxford Gardens looking east from the early 1900s (top) and today (bottom)

management of many run-down houses. By 1960 the independent shops of Notting Hill Gate's thriving high street had been swept away and two characterless blocks loomed over the much widened road. Fifteen years later it was the turn of the northern edge to be torn in two as the Westway displaced many residents whilst those left behind in areas such as Acklam Road endured four years of construction horror.

The building of houses and the railway attracted labourers searching for work and a strong Irish community had long been established when they were joined in the 1930s by Spanish immigrants fleeing their civil war and then Caribbeans sailing to a new life on the Empire Windrush. It was their love for street parties which saw the first Notting Hill Carnival take place in 1965, since when it has grown into a two day colourful extravaganza enjoyed by the hundreds of thousands who throng the crowded streets. Whilst the weekly Norland Market now lies under the wheels of vehicles driving on the West Cross Route by Shepherd's Bush roundabout, the costermongers of Portobello Road's market have been joined by antique dealers and become a popular tourist destination, as has the famous blue door featured in the film *Notting Hill*.

The transformation of seventeenth century Knottynghull from rural countryside to the place we know today has at times been controversial but always interesting and has created one of the most desirable places to live in west London. Where deer once roamed now wide tree-lined residential roads are found alongside streets with shops offering an eclectic range of goods and restaurants serving dishes which reflect the multi-cultural mix of the people who now live and work here and call Notting Hill home.

Caroline MacMillan
www.westlondonwalks.co.uk

Below: Portobello Road looking north at the junction of Westbourne Park taken early last century (top) and today (bottom).

Top right: Snowdrops **Bottom left:** Echinops **Bottom right:** Tulips

Ladbroke Square Garden

Included in the plans for the Ladbroke Estate when it was built in the mid-nineteenth century were sixteen crescent gardens or squares solely for the use of residents of the houses surrounding them. They could access the 'pleasure ground' or 'paddock' as they were originally known through a gate in the fence which separated their rear garden from the private communal one.

Measuring seven acres, Ladbroke Square is the largest garden on the Ladbroke Estate. Roads run round three of its sides, on the northern edge the mansions' rear gardens lead into the communal one. The garden feels like a maze with smaller paths leading off the formal Broad Walk and into three lawned areas, hidden from each other by shrubberies and a myriad of trees. The central lawn possesses some magnificent oaks, a rose bower has been erected on the east lawn and a mulberry tree planted on the west one to mark the Queen's Silver Jubilee in 1977.

After many years the old fountain was removed. The remaining round bed containing the new slate sphere, created by renowned sculptor Joe Smith, is a colourful joy of herbaceous plants throughout the year, with seasonal under-planting and climbing roses blooming round the original urns. The Victorian summer house has been carefully restored, a children's play area is tucked behind trees and for the energetic there is a tennis court. The full-time gardener lives in his charming brick cottage located in the north east corner of the garden and last year saw the unveiling of a brand new water-fountain, designed by the noted sculptor and Garden Member, Nigel Hall RA, hewn from a single lump of granite.

Finally, it is with enormous sadness that the Ladbroke Square Garden Committee have reported the death of Henrietta Phipps. She was a Member of the Committee and its Honorary Secretary for very many years and, following her decision to retire from the Committee in 2012, she became a Trustee of the Ladbroke Square Garden Trust. Henrietta was one of the longest-standing Garden members and her in-depth knowledge of, and passion for, the Garden and its history was unsurpassed.

A huge thanks to Sonja and Sarah from the Ladbroke Square Garden Committee
and Colin the head gardener for helping me with this project.

Top left: Holly
Top right: The new water fountain
Bottom right: Honesty

Top: Tulips
Bottom left: Daffodils
Opposite: Bluebells

Previous page 21:
Rose (top left) and Iris (bottom left)

Top left: Banksia Rose

Bottom left: Dog Rose, Rosa Canina

Left: Horse Chestnut

Top right: Soldier Beetle

Bottom right: Stamens from an Elfin Pink Beard Tongue

Kensington Park Road

Plans for the first six large detached houses built in 1844 in Kensington Park Road were displayed at the Royal Academy, they were individually designed with one named Swiss Villa and companions similarly named Italian, Elizabethan and Norman.

Overleaf bottom left: Stanley Gardens

Overleaf bottom right and page 27: Kensington Park Gardens

KENSINGTON PARK ROAD

Elgin Crescent

Elgin Crescent was originally known as Elgin Road and over the years has been home to many famous people including Jawaharlal Nehru, the first Prime Minister of India, Sir Osbert Lancaster and Sir Laurence Olivier.

Left, opposite and inset: There are clearly a lot of Americans living in and around Elgin Crescent as the effort they made for Hallowe'en in 2015 was impressive.

Bottom right: Female Blackcap

Arundel & Elgin Gardens

Arundel and Elgin Gardens is one of the few to retain its original planting layout. In recent years there has been a continuous programme of replacing dead trees, additional ones added and an increase to the diversity of species in the gardens.

The garden is dominated by a huge central plane tree and has a particularly wonderful display of cherry blossom in the spring. Although the complex mid-19th century path layout has been simplified some of the original internal railings survive. Residents enjoy the garden's informality and the lawns, backed by beds of flowering shrubs, gives them plenty of sun bathing space whilst the highlight of the annual summer party is the Arundel vs. Elgin tug-of-war.

Thank you to Tassy MacInnes from the Garden Committee, who kindly let me through her house to photograph the garden during the past year.

Top left: Acer

Opposite: Goldfinch
Top left: Euphorbia
Middle left: Tulip Ballerina
Bottom left: Forget-me-not

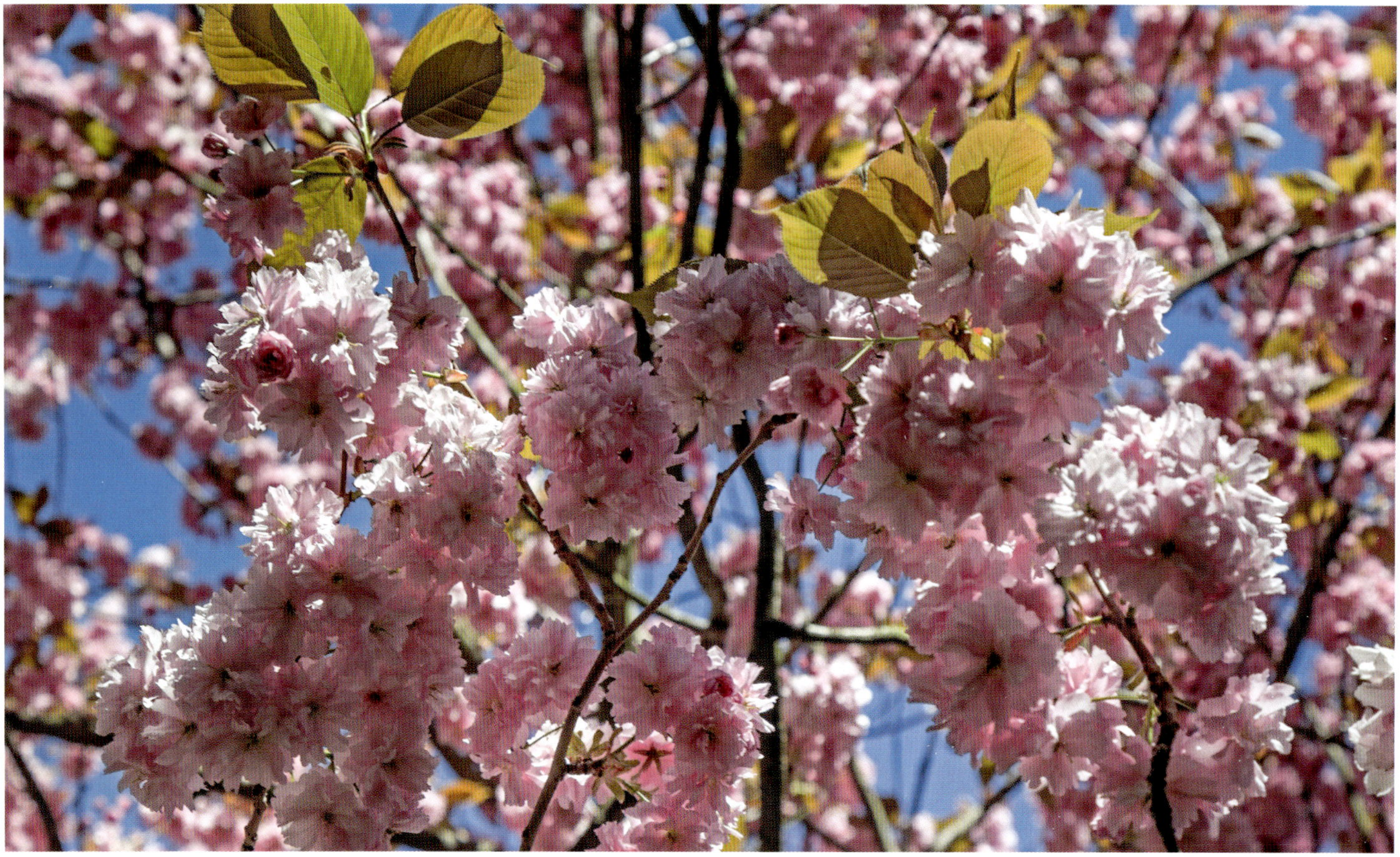

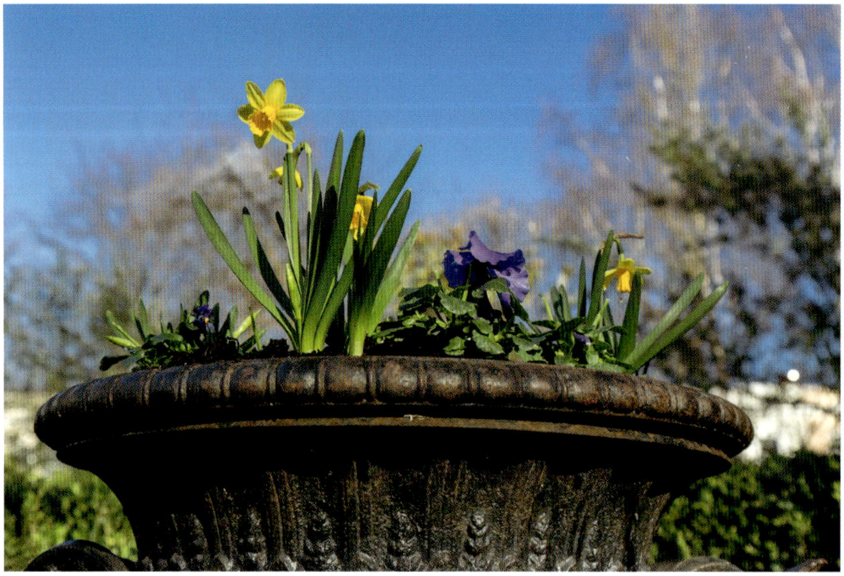

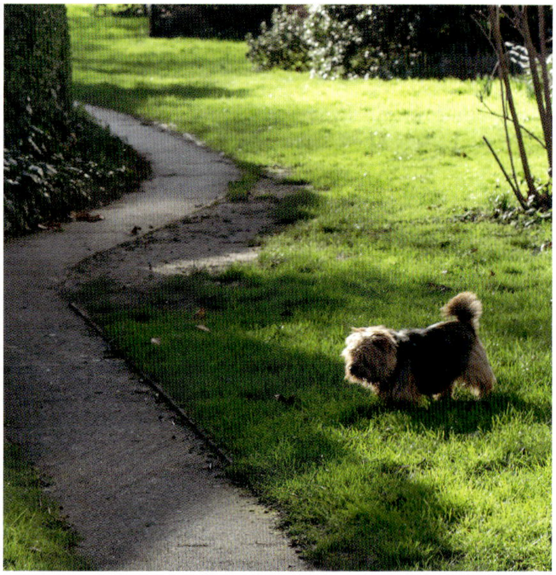

Opposite top:
Cherry Blossom

Opposite bottom left:
Daffodils and Pansies

Top: Plane Tree

Middle right:
Garden Orb Spider

Bottom right:
Climbing Rose

St John's Church

With its soaring spire St. John's was built on the hill used by spectators as a natural grandstand to view the ill-fated Hippodrome race-course. Now a listed building, it forms the centre point of the Ladbroke Estate.

40

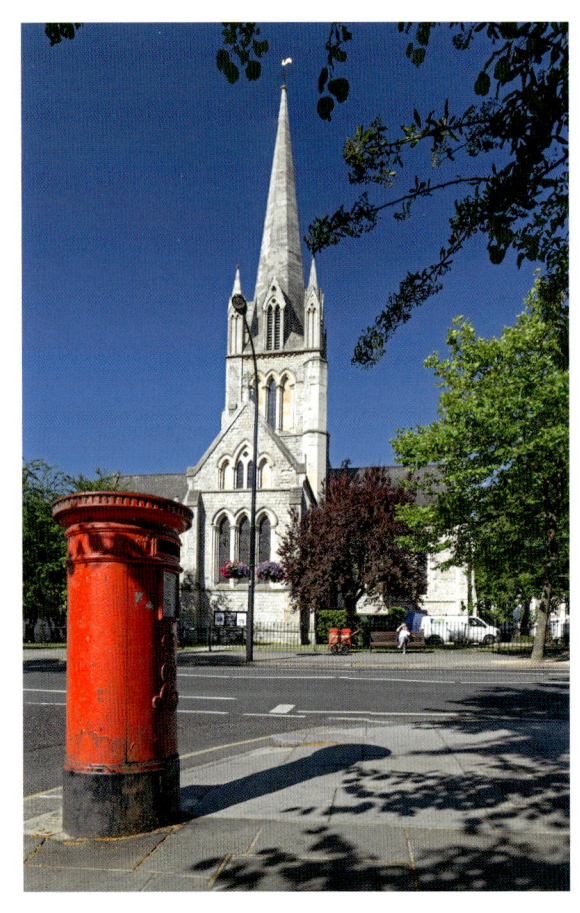

Notting
Hill
MAY
FAIR
Saturday, 21st May, 1-5pm
St John's Church, Lansdowne Crescent, W11
Dog Show: 2.30pm, Fancy Dress Contest: 3.30pm
Maypole Dancing
Coconut Shy, Bouncy Castle, Barbecue, Cakes,
Cream Teas, Bric-a-Brac, Plants, Raffle

Tagalog Mass
St. John's
NOTTING HILL
SUNDAY SERVICES
DAILY SERVICES
PARISH
EUCHARIST
10.30am
Pearl

A walk around west Notting Hill

TIME: 1 HOUR 15 MINUTES

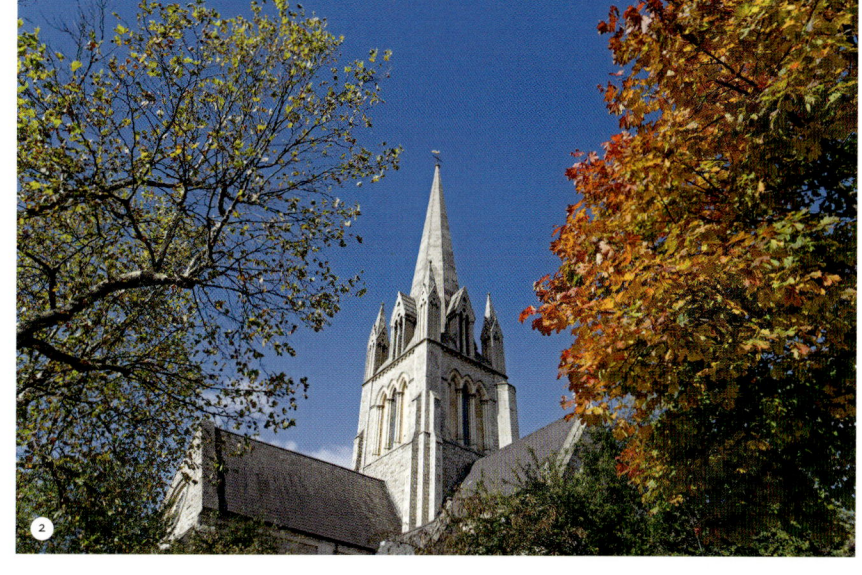

The walk starts at Holland Park tube station which opened in 1900. It was envisaged that a hotel would be built on top of the flat roof but this has never happened. Turn immediately left into Lansdowne Road, across the street stands Lansdowne House (1) which was also built in 1900 as six individual apartments, each with a north-lit two storey studio and the blue plaque records the names of some former artist residents. As you walk up the hill admire the splendid houses which James Weller Ladbroke commissioned architect Thomas Allason to build on his estate in the 1840s.

Go right into St. John's Gardens and on reaching the church, turn to admire the view down the hill of John Whyte's famous Hippodrome Racecourse where steeplechases were held for four years from 1837. When built in 1845 St. John's (2) was known as 'The Church in the Hayfields' so you can imagine the rural aspect then. With the church behind you bear right and glance at the number of Ones (3) for house number 1, then first left into Lansdowne Crescent where there is a splendid telephone box in the front garden of one house and first left again into Lansdowne Rise which was previously called Montpelier Road. Pass 1930's Lansdowne Court and go first right on the opposite side of the road which takes you back into Lansdowne Road with its terraces of softly coloured houses. Turn first left into short Rosmead Road (4) and peep into the private garden on your right which featured in the film *Notting Hill*.

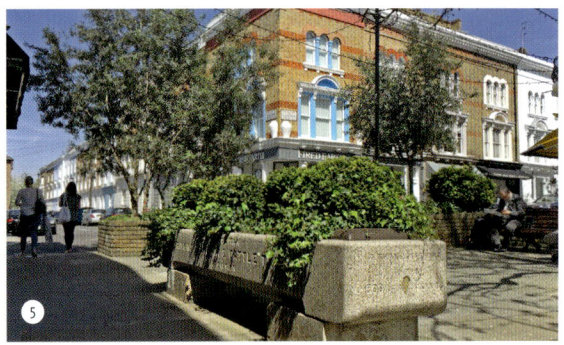

At the junction bear left into Elgin Crescent, number 143 has a delightful mural by Hugo Dalton called *Morning Glory*. The road merges into Clarendon Road, cross it to reach the former Clarendon Hotel with its distinctive columns of tiles on the corner with Portland Road, it is now the Octavia Housing Lunch Club. Continue down Portland Road past the watchful lion heads over the doorway on your right, the road bends to the left and takes you to the pedestrianised area of Clarendon Cross. Clarendon Works on the left was originally a brick factory and has recently been transformed into a contemporary private house. The inscriptions each end of the 1878 cattle trough (5) are hard to decipher but one reads "A Righteous Man Regardeth the Life of his Beast" and the other "A Thank Offering to the God of all Mercies".

Walk down short Hippodrome Place whose name is a reminder you are now standing in the middle of John Whyte's folly of a racecourse, the soil on which he built it is heavy clay so after rain the going got very heavy. Reaching Walmer Road, just to your right is the last of the many pottery kilns (6) once found in this area, a plaque recounts the history; Avondale Park opposite is the only large space open to the local public because all the other gardens are gated and only for the residents whose houses overlook them. The Earl of Zetland on the corner of Pottery Lane is yet another pub which has ceased to serve beer but it was open when David Hemmings drove by in the 1966 film 'Blow Up'. Enjoy walking down Pottery Lane (7) which two hundred years ago ran through the notorious Potteries and Piggeries, the Catholic Church of St. Francis of Assisi is tucked in a courtyard on the left. Take the first turning right, cross Princedale Road and so into Penzance Place, the 1984 classrooms of St. Clement and St. James Primary School replace the original 1862 building which burnt down due to an electrical fault. Next door the Islamic Universal Association occupies the former West London Tabernacle which often had more than a thousand worshippers attending evening services. Turn left as you enter St. James's Gardens and follow the square round, stopping to read the sign outside Lewis Vulliamy's church. The letterbox on the corner of Addison Avenue dates back to Victorian times whilst a stone on the wall between numbers 1 and 2 St. James's Gardens announces it was the first house built in the square. After passing the Spanish and Portuguese Synagogue, turn left into St. Ann's Villas (8) with their charming diagonal brick work and stone facings, they were once known as the Red Villas and on number 17 there is a blue plaque to Albert Onesime Britannicus Gwathveoyd Louis Chevalier, born here in 1861 and who became better known as the music hall comedian Albert Chevalier.

When crossing Queensdale Road glance down to the right, the building with golden domes near the end started life in 1859 as the Baptist Norland Chapel, became Norland Castle when the Salvation Army took it over twenty years later and is now the Sikh Temple. Take the right turn into elegant Royal Crescent, laid out in 1846 by Robert Cantwell and reminiscent of its namesake in Bath. At the junction of busy Holland Park Avenue turn left but pause at the bus pull-in to read the plaque over the drinking fountain erected to the memory of Miss Mary Cray Ratray. Where the Hilton Hotel stands on the opposite side of the road there was once a large roller skating rink. Continue up the leafy avenue, Norland Square is a reminder of the long gone Norland House and estate and the recent notice on the square's railings tells you their history. Numbers 130 and 132 are the only houses in this part of the avenue whose front gardens have not been built over and Old Well House (9) is so called as it is on the site of Benjamin Vulliamy's famous artesian well and in 1794 you could buy a pail filled with his water for one halfpenny. Sir Gilbert Scott's iconic telephone box at the junction with Princedale Road is now Grade II listed, he based the design on the tomb of another great architect, Sir John Soane. Before ending your walk at Holland Park tube station, admire the splendid green tiles of Charrington's Castle pub which opened in the 19th century and retains much of its original interior.

Walk devised by Caroline MacMillan
www.westlondonwalks.co.uk

46 **Top right:** Crocus **Bottom right:** Tulips **Bottom left:** Acanthus mollis

Arundel & Ladbroke Gardens

A nother steeply sloping communal garden, the nineteenth century path layout weaves its way past mature spreading plane and horse chestnut trees which are now under-planted by small flowering trees and woodland shrubs. Some of the original internal railings have also survived the test of time.
On an 1871 map showing the development of Notting Hill, Ladbroke Gardens earned the nickname of 'Coffin Row' as due to various financial crises building work was halted for some time leaving houses in a far from finished state.

Thank you to one of the residents, Lawrence Greenough,
for kindly agreeing to let me in to view the garden.

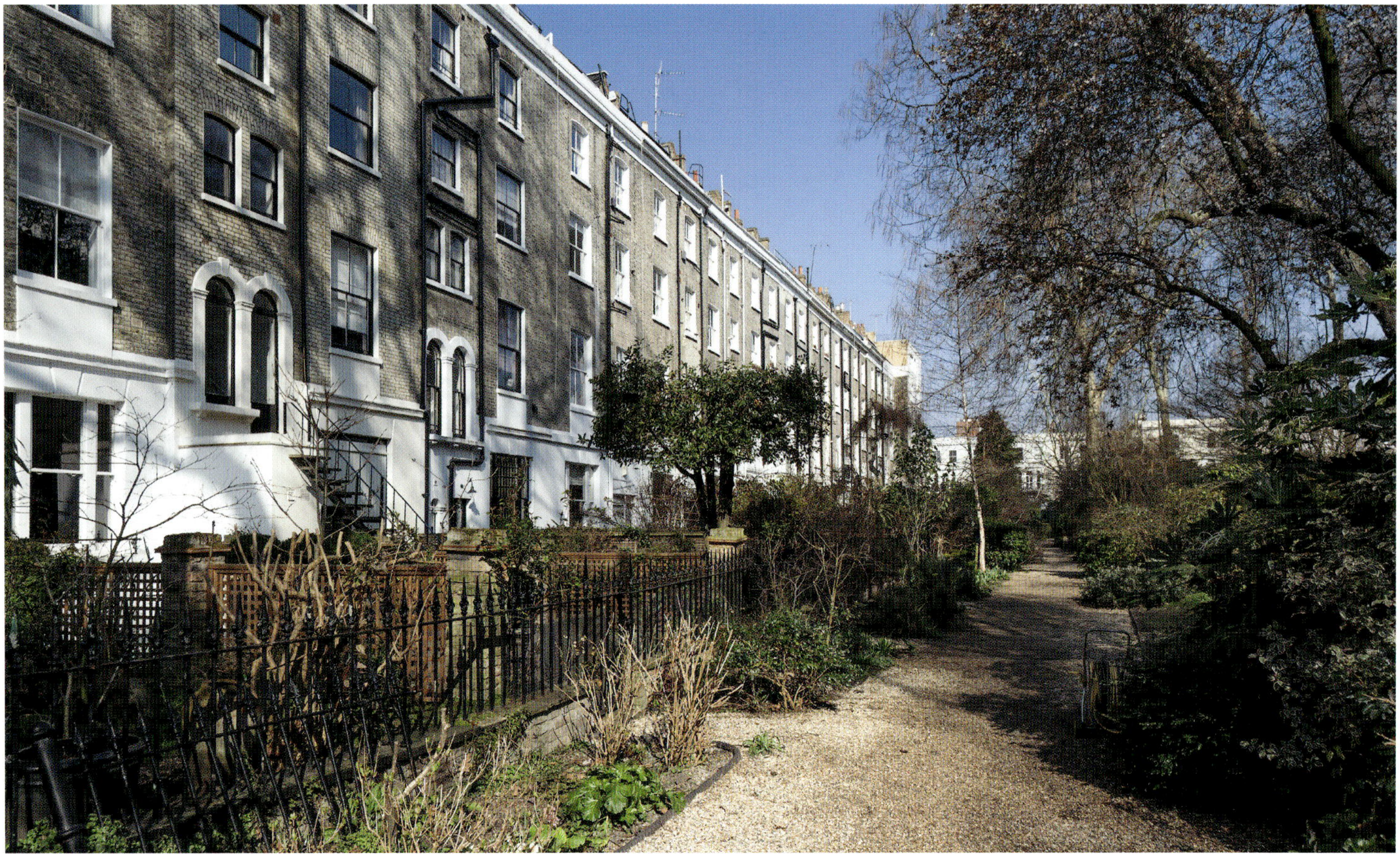

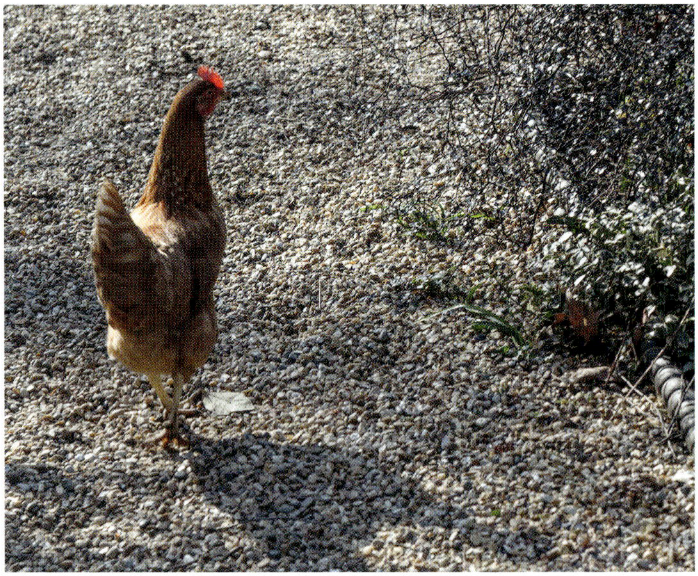

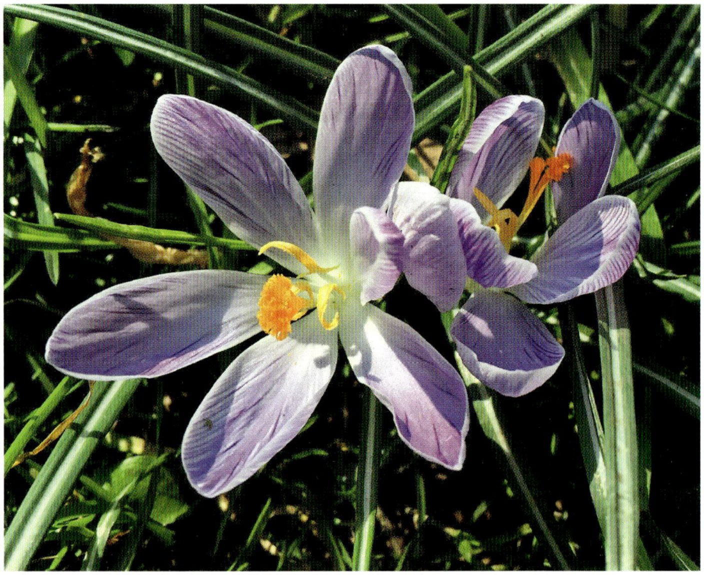

Opposite bottom right:
Crocus

Top: Tulips

Bottom right:
Forget-me-not

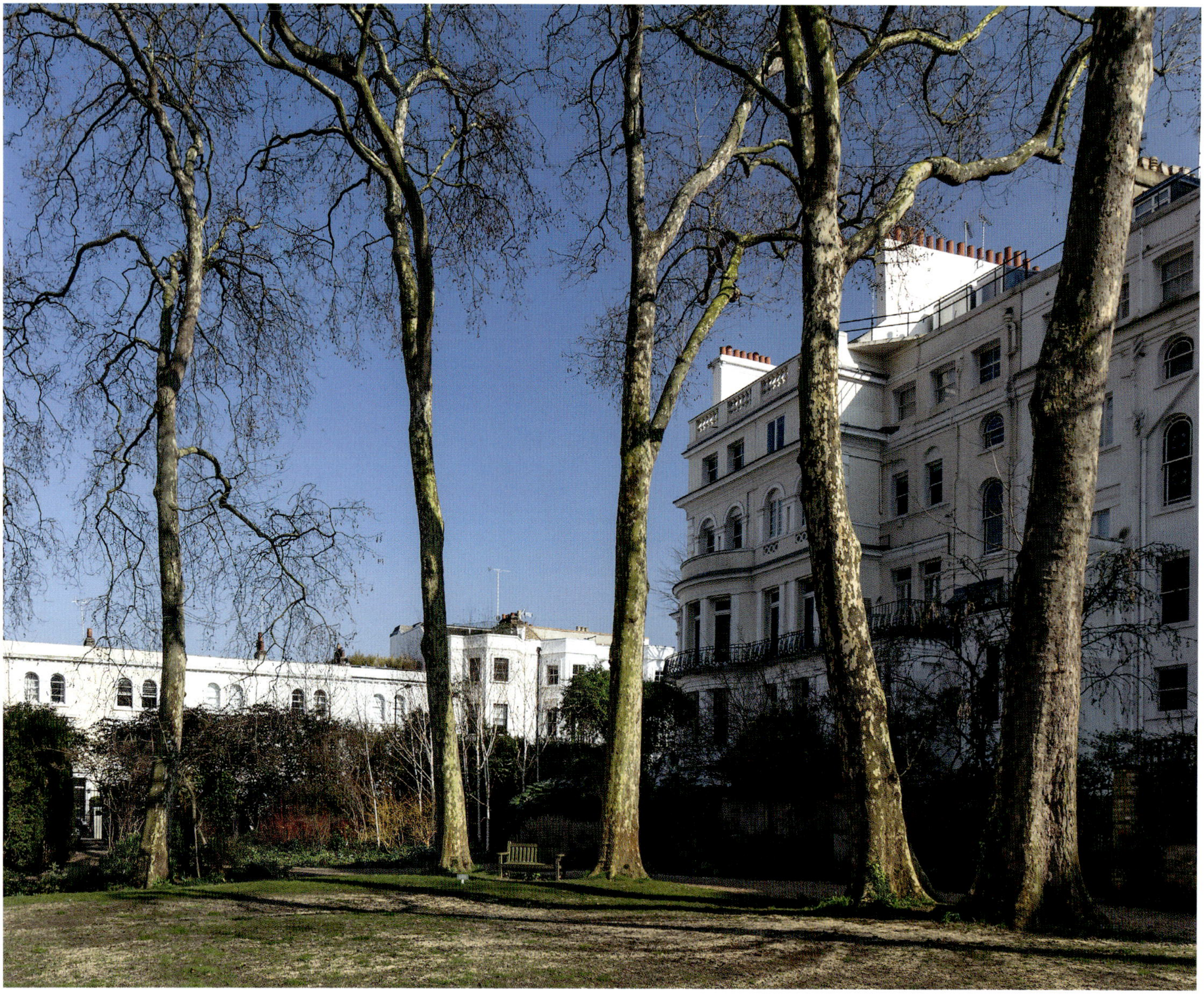

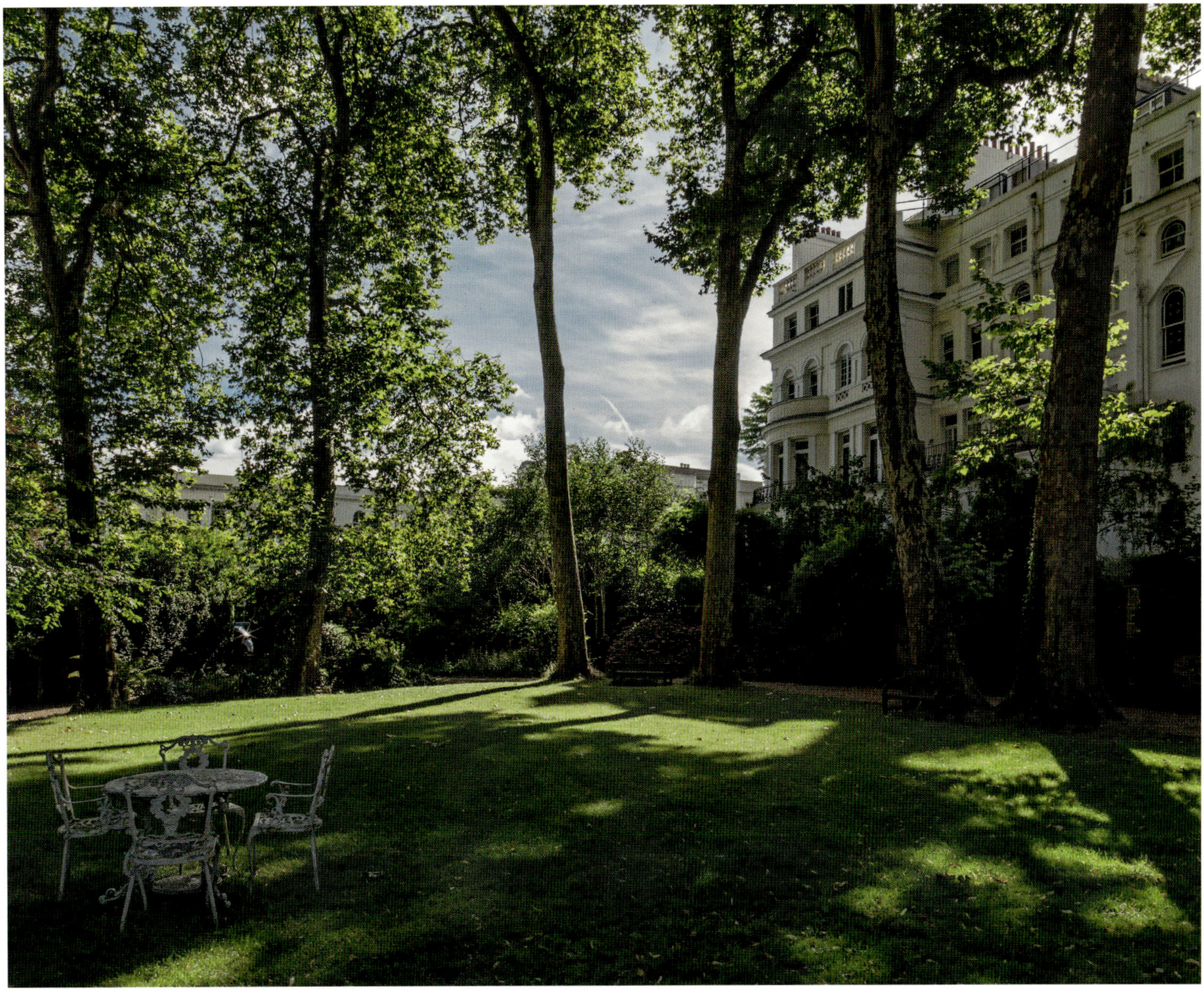

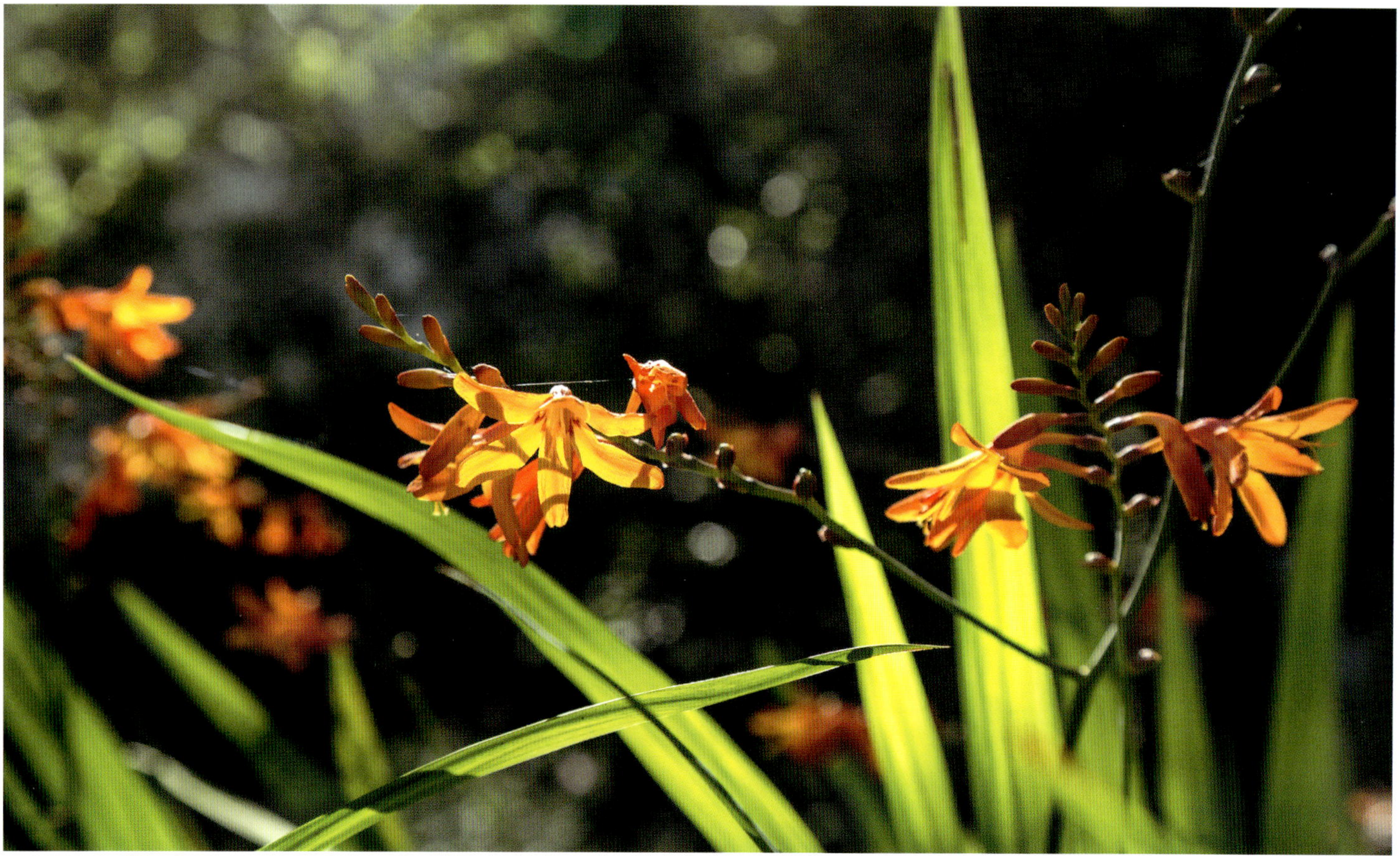

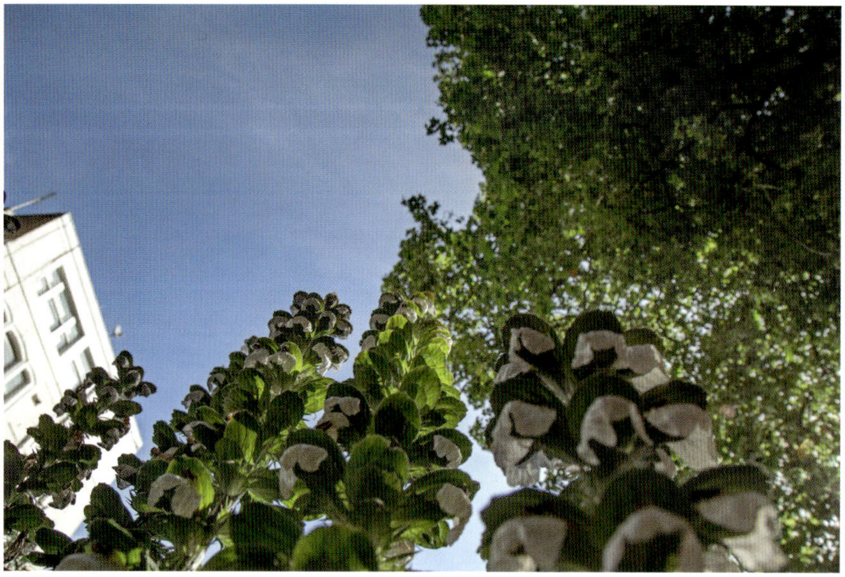

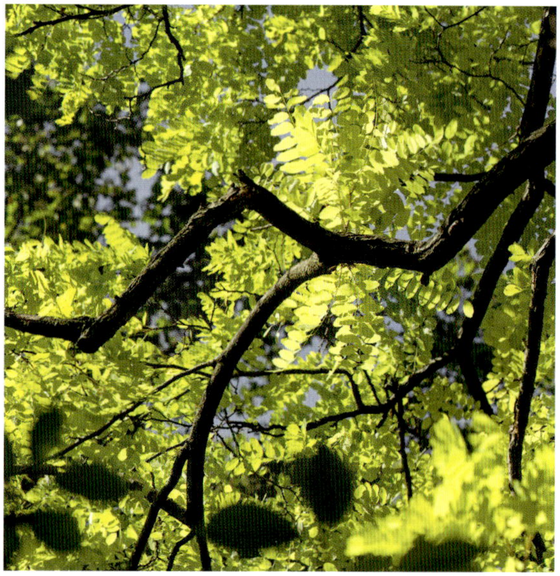

Opposite top: Crocosmia
Opposite bottom right: Robinia
Opposite bottom left and above: Acanthus mollis
Top right: Lobelia 'Hadspen Purple'
Bottom right: Catalpa

Lansdowne Crescent

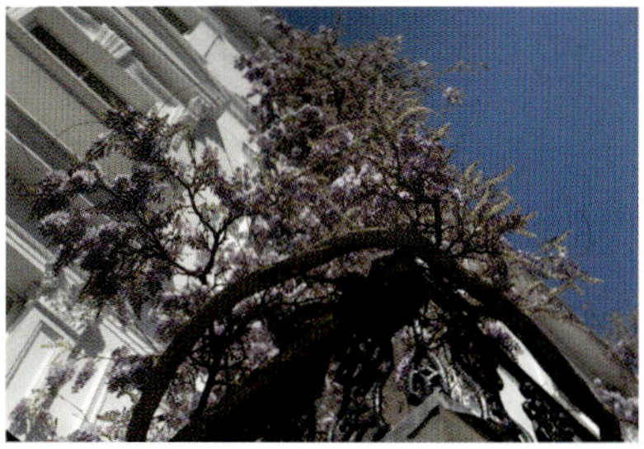

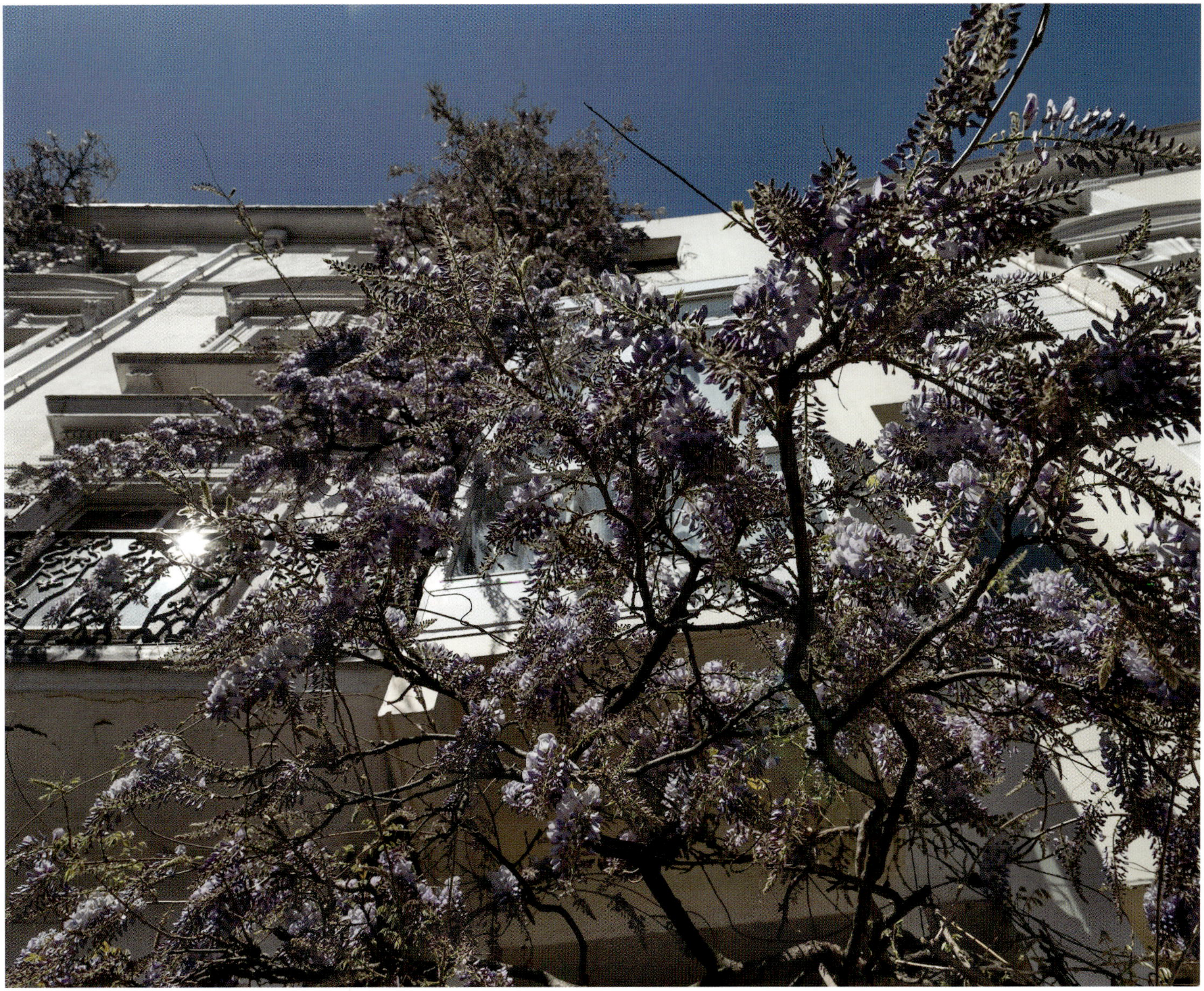

Lansdowne Road

The south end of Lansdowne Road was once called Great Circus Street or Liddiard's Road.

Westbourne Grove

Far left: Westbourne Grove Church: Starting as a Baptist chapel in 1853 the current gothic Victorian church was extended in 1866 and had a seating capacity of 1500. The total cost of the site and building work came to £11,974.

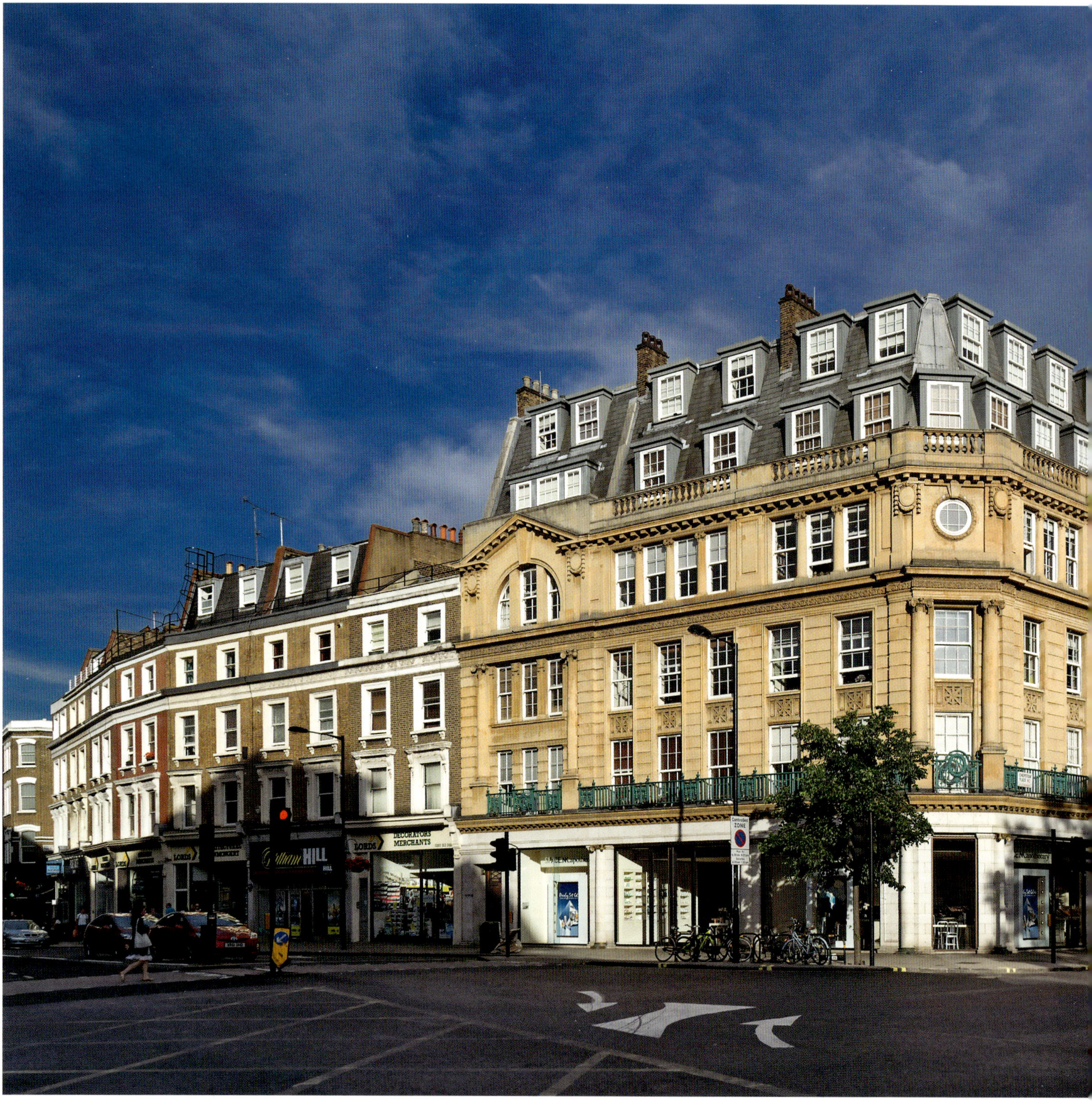
DECORATORS
MERCHANTS
LORDS
HILL

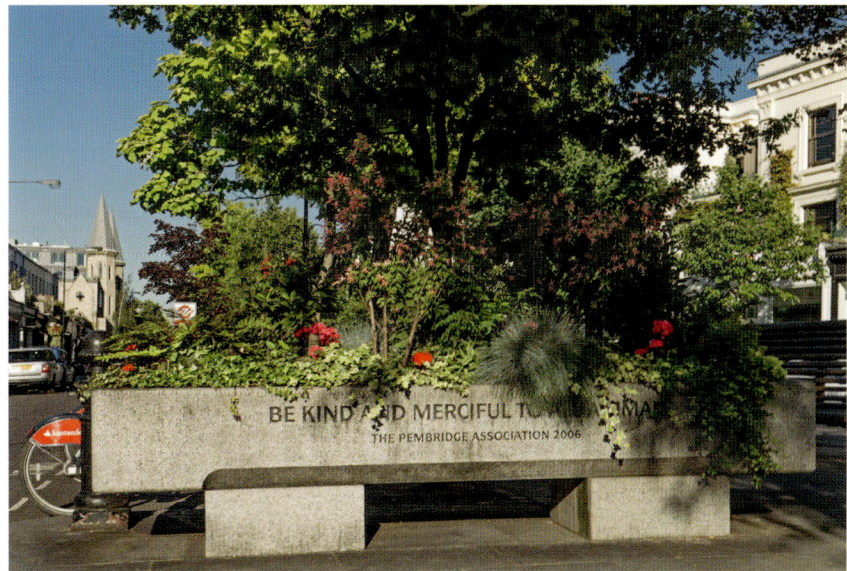

Left: Bradley and Son opened on the corner of Westbourne Grove and Chepstow Place in 1911 and between the wars was regarded as one of the finest couture houses in London. King Edward VII's coronation robes were fashioned here and other celebrated clients included the Tsar of Russia.

A blue plaque at 152 Westbourne Grove reminds us that in 1926 the novelist A. J. Cronin opened his medical practice here.

Westbourne Grove takes its name from Westbourne Green (see the old map on the inside front cover), a former Anglo-Saxon settlement to the west of a bourne or stream, which eventually became the River Westbourne.

Until 1840 Westbourne Grove was a real grove, a lane flanked by tall trees and with banks of wild flowers. It was first known as Archer Street, acquiring its current name in 1938.

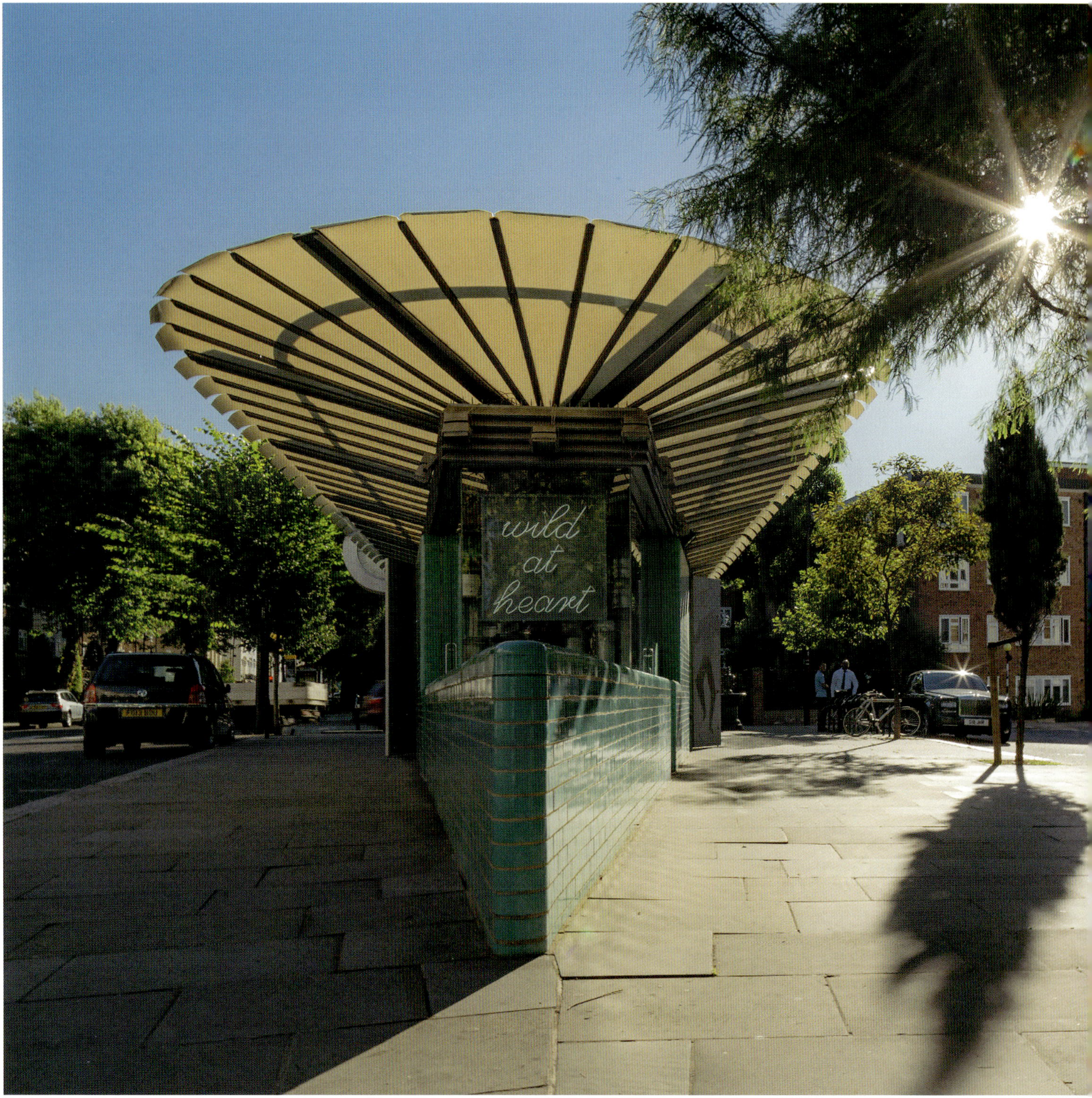
wild
at
heart

Left: What must be the poshest public toilets in West London are those designed by Piers Gough on Turquoise Island in Westbourne Grove. Despite outrage from some residents at the appearance of the quirky loo and florist building on their local traffic island, it has won several awards and now sits well amongst surrounding trendy outlets.

66 **Top left:** Bluebells **Top right:** Female Blackbird **Bottom left:** Agapanthus

Lansdowne & Clarendon Garden

One of the earliest to be laid out on the estate around 1860, this open one acre garden is scattered with mature trees surrounded by borders of beautiful flowering shrubs. In the centre is a grove of birch trees which replace a central shrub bed originally connected to the perimeter path by cross paths.

As I've been photographing several of the Ladbroke Estate gardens through the seasons I have been most struck by how few butterflies that I have seen, this garden being the exception. However, I was very pleased to have spotted a green woodpecker, who are notoriously shy.

Thanks to local resident, Neville Buch, for allowing me to capture the garden throughout the past year.

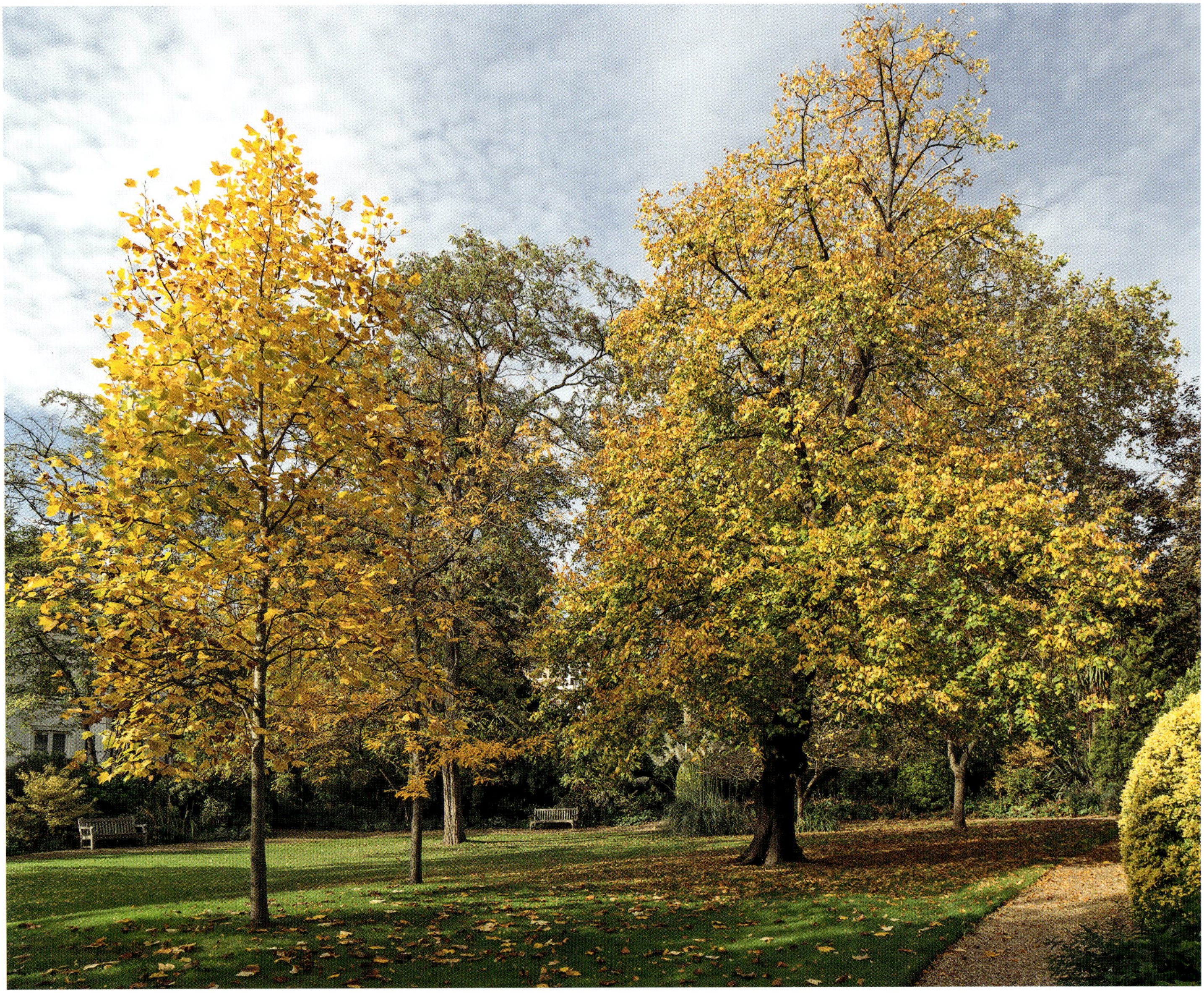

Top left: Great Tit leaving its nest
Bottom left: Common Blue Butterfly

Right: European Green Woodpecker

Opposite bottom right: Hover Fly on a Daisy

Opposite bottom left: Agapanthus

Overleaf: Crocus (bottom left) and Boston, the Airedale Terrier (bottom right)

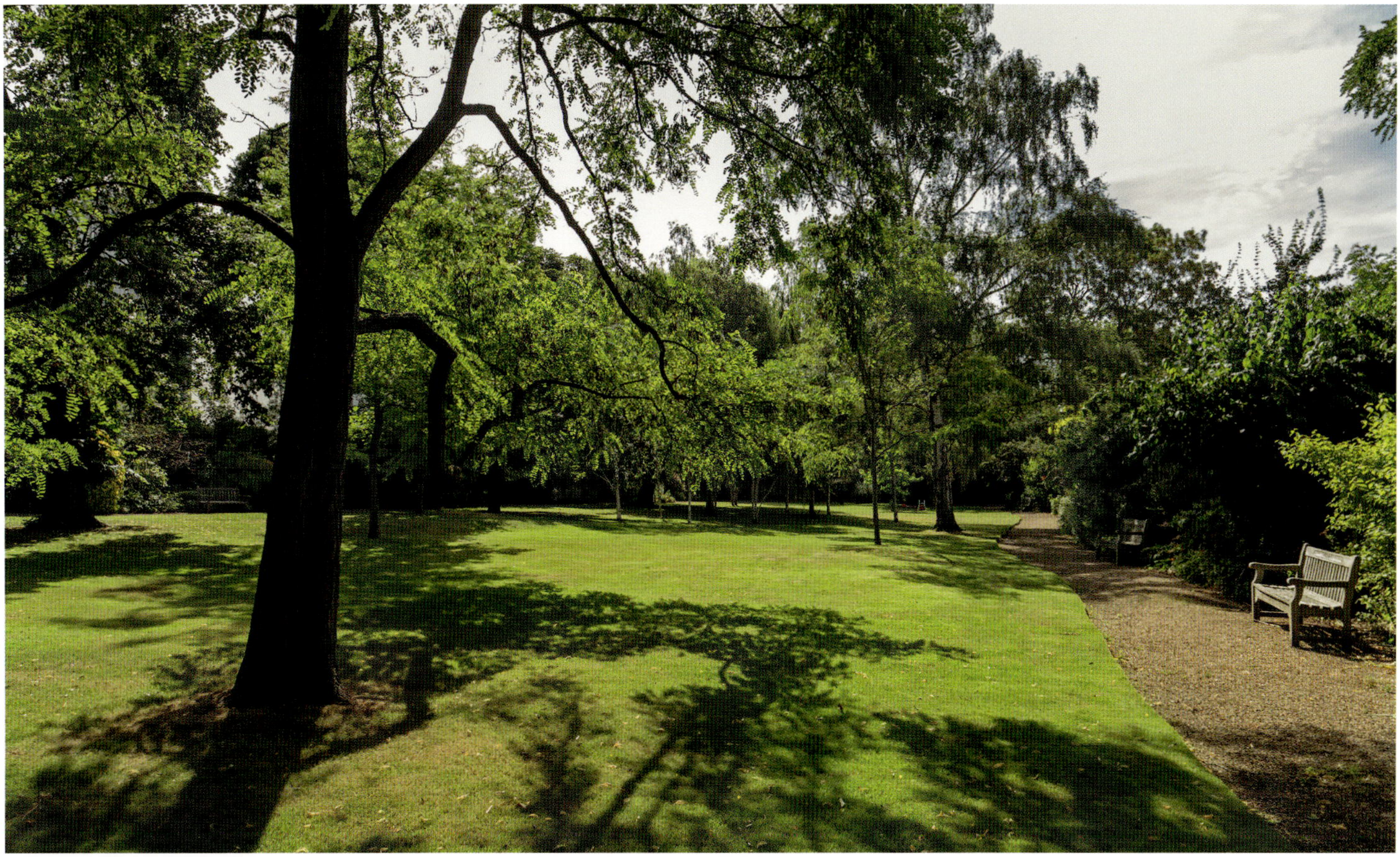

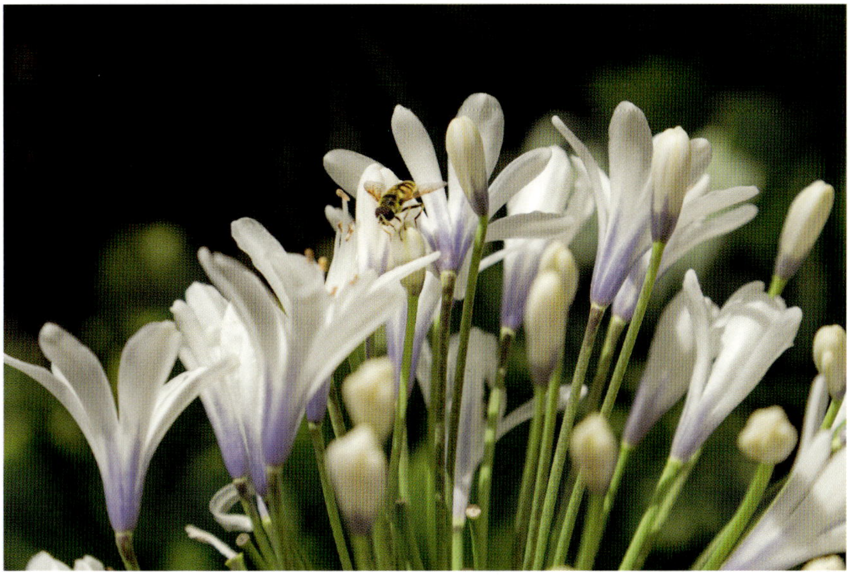

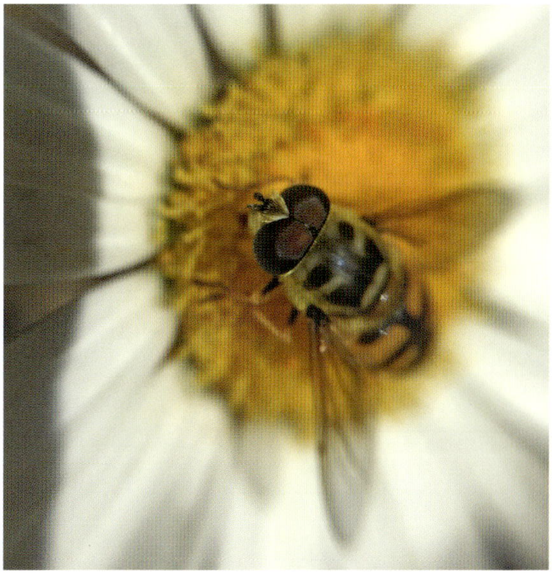

72

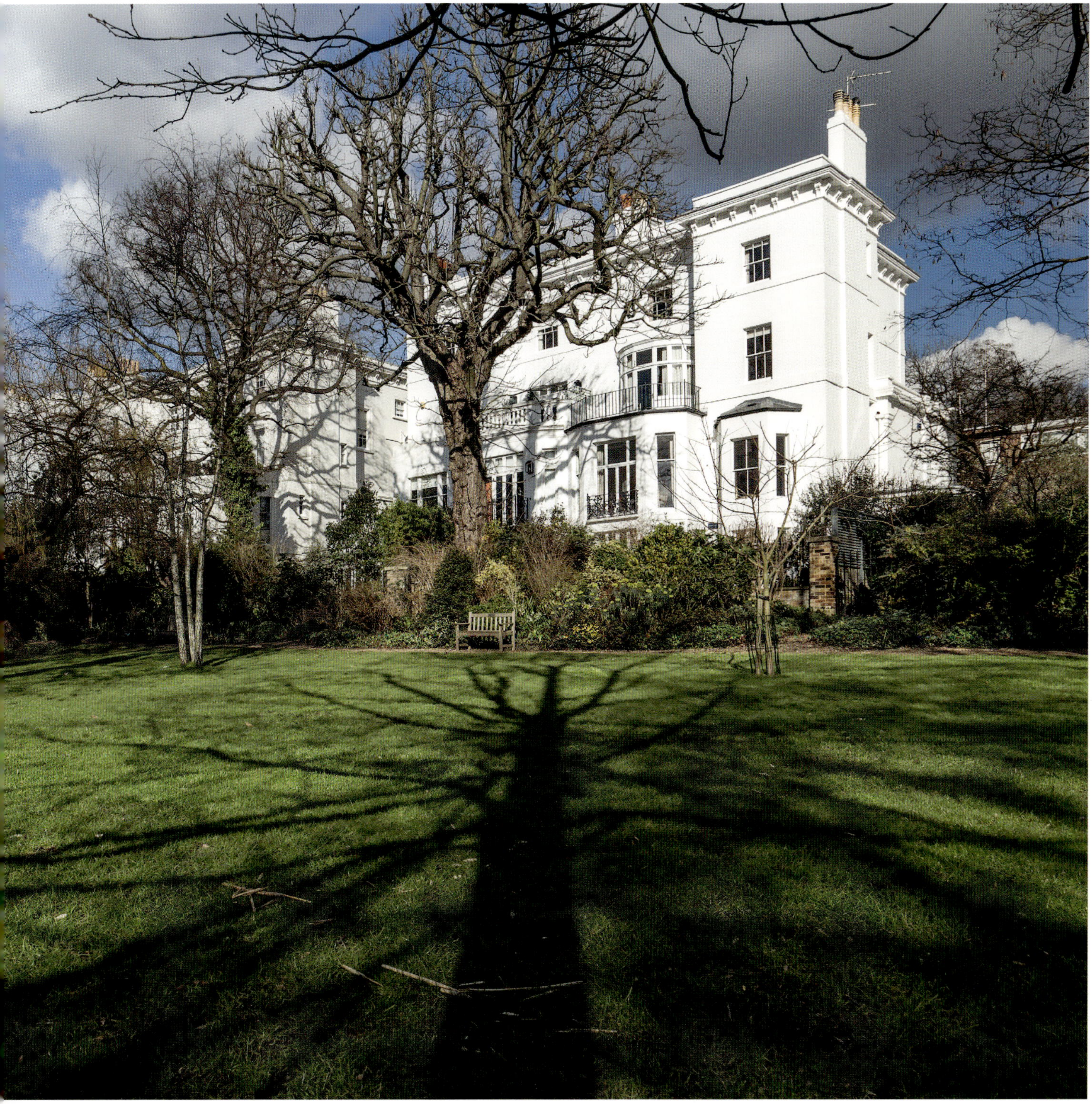

Portobello Market

Once a country track from Notting Hill Gate to a lone farm in rural north Kensington, Green Lane was renamed Portobello Road in honour of Admiral Vernon's great victory at Porto Bello in 1739. When the first cottages were built at the southern end near the Sun in Splendour in 1851 there were still cornfields and meadowland on either side of The Lane, as locals referred to it, and the tranquil silence would be broken by the songs of soaring larks during the day and nightingales as dusk fell.

Top and bottom right: Shops in Blenheim Crescent just off Portobello Road

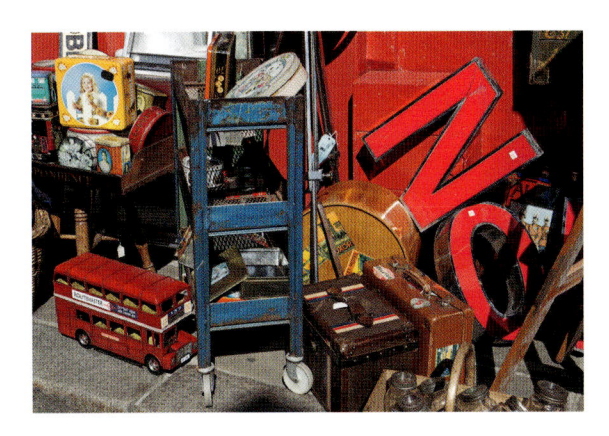

BOOKS for COOKS
The SHOP for ALL COOKS
EST

fresh from
OYSTER BAR
the west of ireland
BEN BRIERLEY
RARE BOOKS
07768 058 632
ANTIQUE
WATCHES MUSICAL BOXES
ANTIQUE 101 ARCADE

The Duke of Wellington
PEDESTRIAN ZONE

By the late 19th century a Saturday market selling fresh produce had sprung up on Portobello Road. Soon they were joined by totters with their bric-a-brac with antique dealers arriving in the 1940s. A myriad of shops opened along both sides of the road and the street stalls began trading on a daily basis.

Right bottom: It was a pleasure to meet Bianca and her handcrafted badges and gifts; she can be found at the market every Saturday.

The interesting mural in Codrington Mews, just off Blenheim Crescent

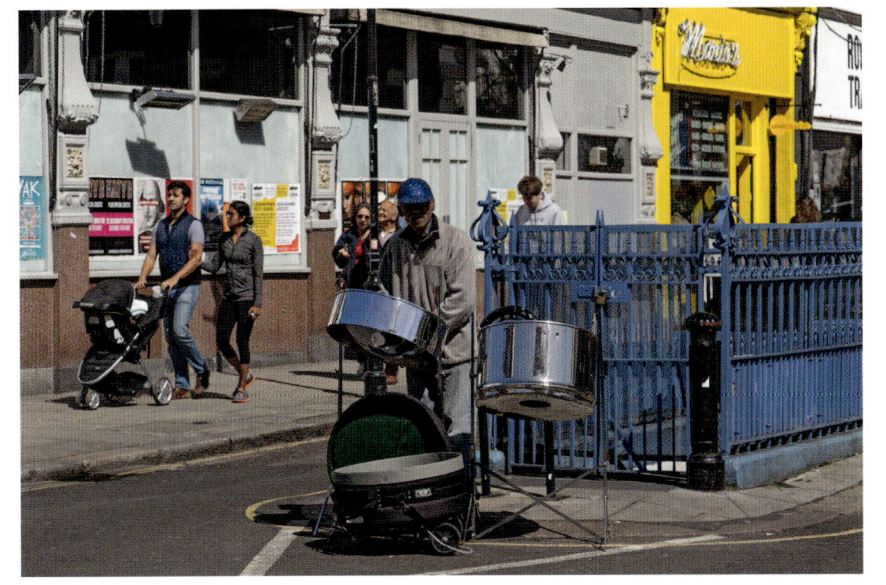

Now one of London's major tourist attractions, Portobello Road together with its unique market continues to retain its own special character.

Notting Hill Carnival

It was in the mid 1960s the West Indian community became involved in a local fete and a mobile steel pan was heard on the streets of Notting Hill for the first time – so the Carnival was born.

Traditional costume bands and colourful floats joined the street parade of brightly dressed performers and by 1975 the event had grown into Britain's biggest street party.

169
Notting Hill
CFC
Halal
حلال
SELECT FOOD & WINE
FRESHLY MADE SANDWICHES
HOT & COLD DRINKS, TOBACCONIST
SPIVACK
CHEMIST
OFF LICENCE

PORTOBELLO ROAD
125B

83

Winkworth
020 7727 3227
Winkworth
020 7727 3227
Winkworth.co.uk
Winkworth.co.uk

Hundreds of thousands now attend the event held over the August Bank Holiday weekend with Sunday traditionally being the family day. The next day more than sixty bands entertain the crowds who pack the streets to watch the parade and enjoy the aromas from the street food stalls selling traditional Caribbean patties, jerk chicken and fried plantain.

Pembridge Square

Wetherby School was founded in Wetherby Place but retained the name when it moved to Pembridge Square in 1971.

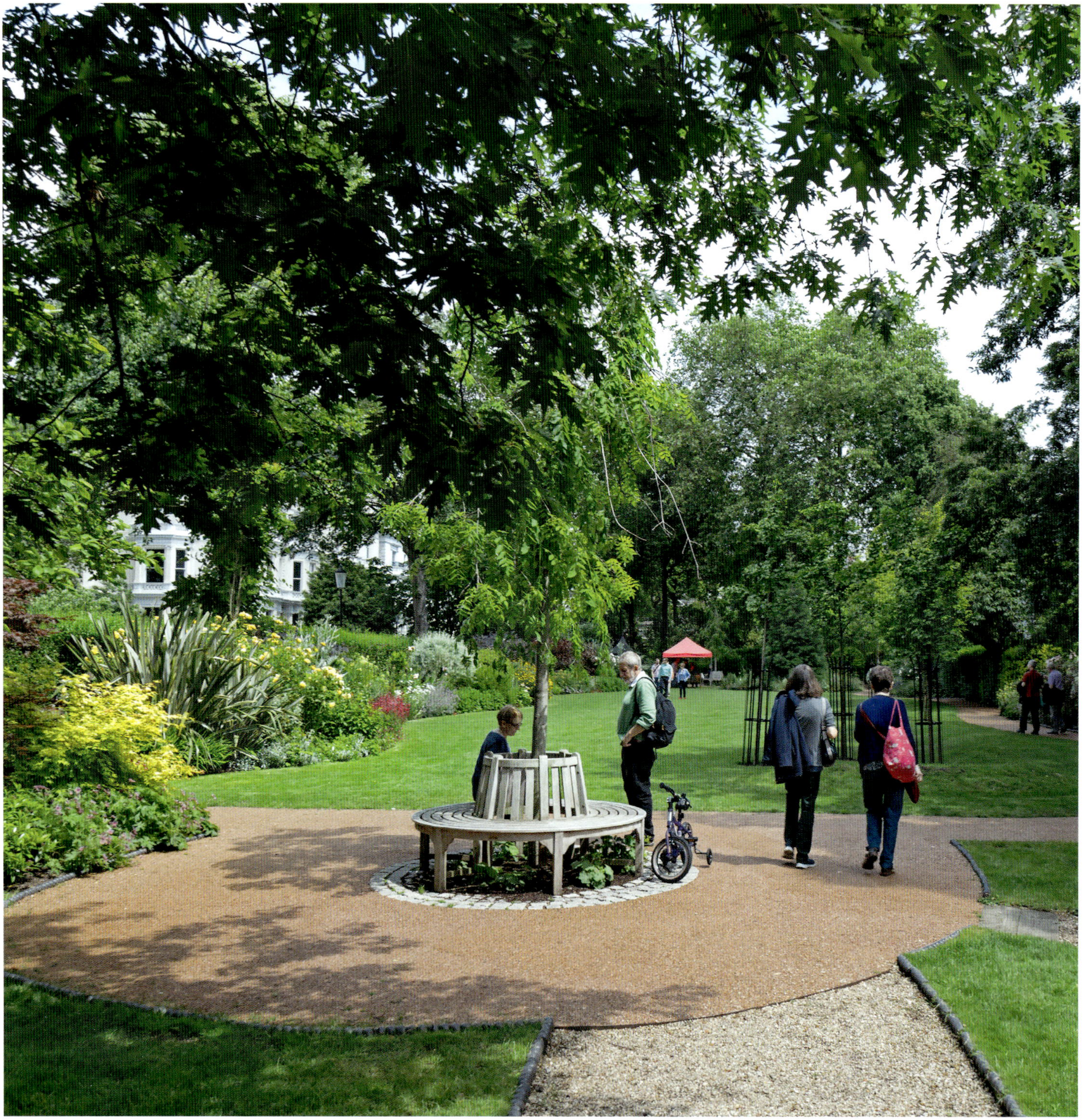

Completed in 1865 Pembridge Square's long rectangular garden has a beautiful woodland area, wild flowers flourish at the east end and a rose garden at the west whilst the long herbaceous border is a joy throughout the year.

Thanks to Jean Lloyd from the garden committee, for allowing me to take these pictures during Open Garden Squares weekend.

Colville Mews

The Union of Ragged Schools opened a school in Colville Mews in 1862 which gave free education to children from poor families. The Union adopted the name after the first schools they opened were attended by children who were raggedly clothed and rarely wore shoes.

Colville Square

Top: The church of All Saints was the project of wealthy Reverend Samuel Walker who planned it as a memorial to his parents and also a centre point for his housing development in and around what became Powis and Colville Squares (opposite page). But his plans were greater than his finances and 'Walker's Folly' had to wait some years before it received a spire which was not as lofty as the one he so admired on Salisbury Cathedral.

Bottom left and right: Colville School, Lonsdale Road

Opening in 1879 as the Buckingham Terrace School, there were strict rules for the teachers.

MALE TEACHERS
- No closely cropped hair
- No rolled or unlinked shirt sleeves

FEMALE TEACHERS
- No bloomers, no showing ankles
- No 10 inch bustle extensions
- No marriage or other unseemly behaviour

All Saints Road

In the late 1960s, All Saints Road was regarded as 'the frontline' to an area controlled by drug dealers. Those heady days have long gone and the road continues to attract musicians to the various music shops and is now known for its cutting edge food and design.

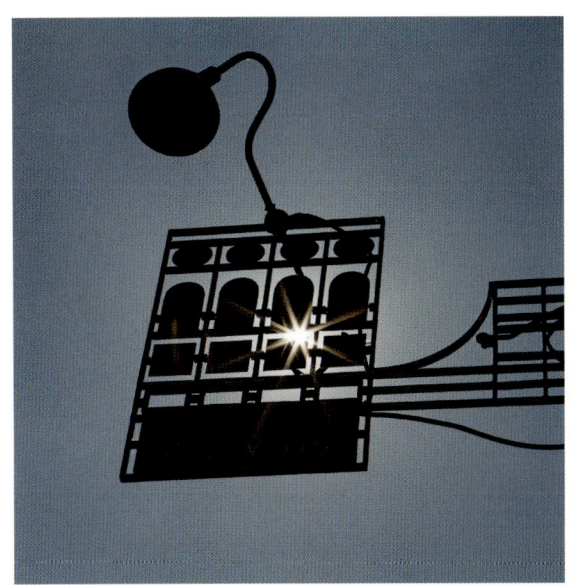

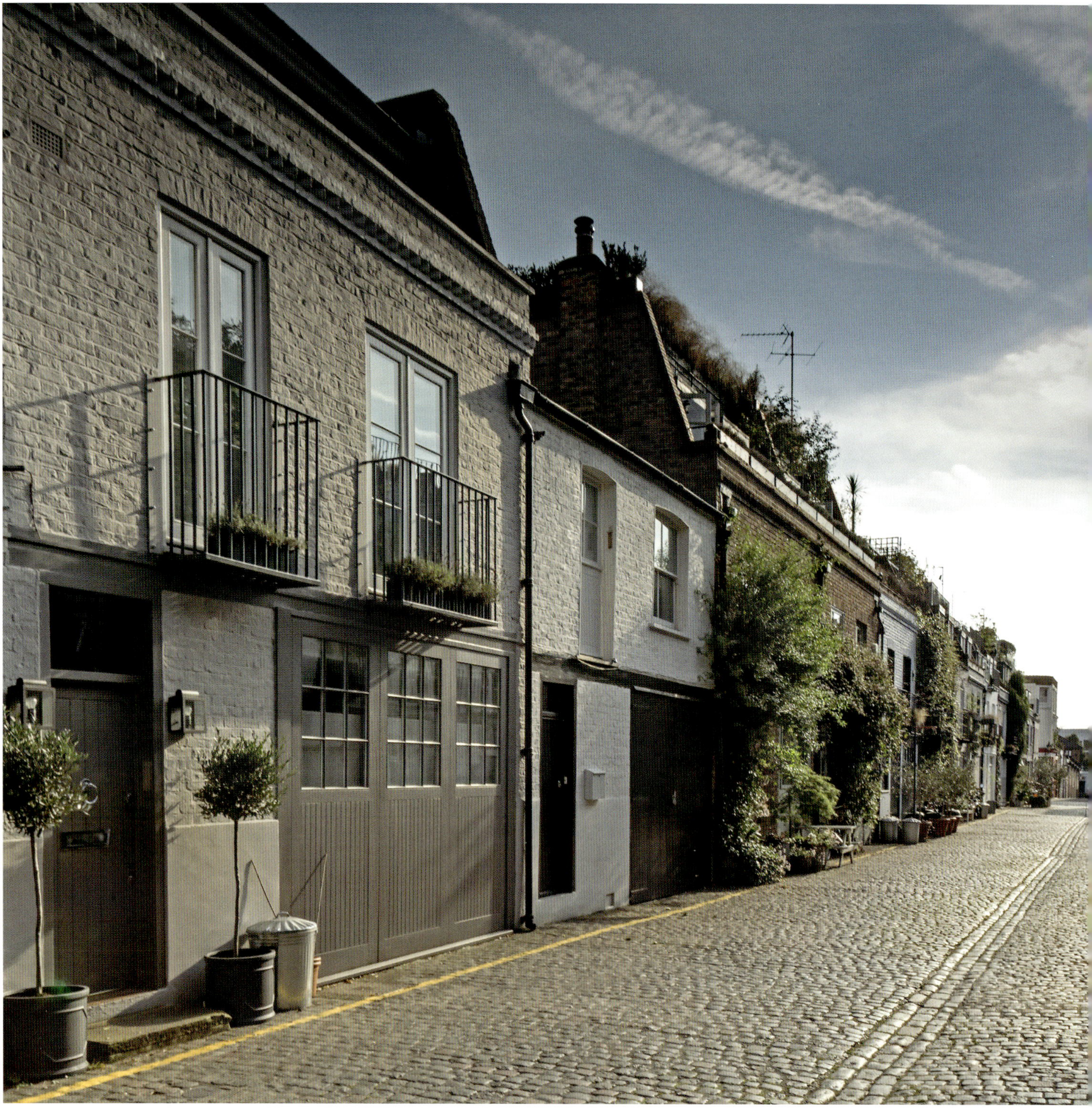

St Luke's Mews: From the 17th century onwards mews were built round paved yards or narrow streets running behind large city houses. The rich owner's horses and carriages were housed on the ground floor with the coachman living above.

98

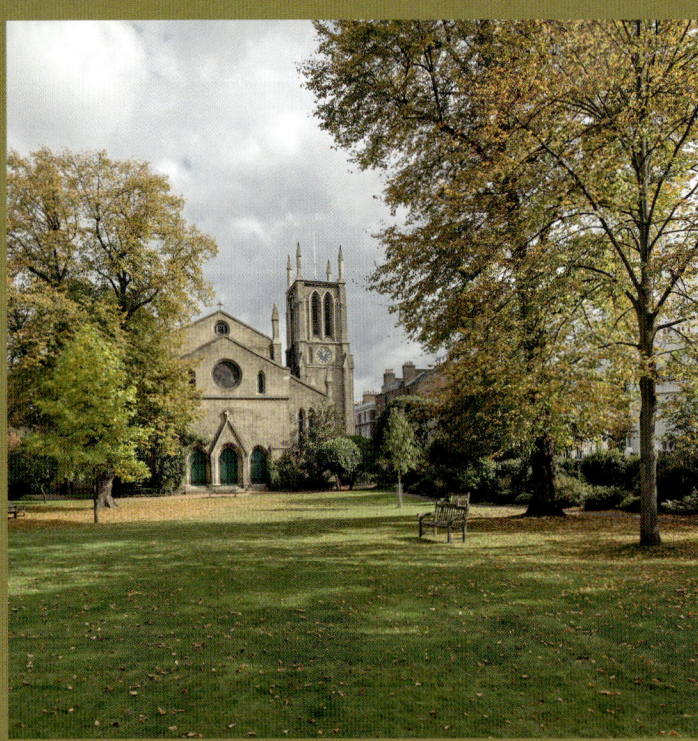

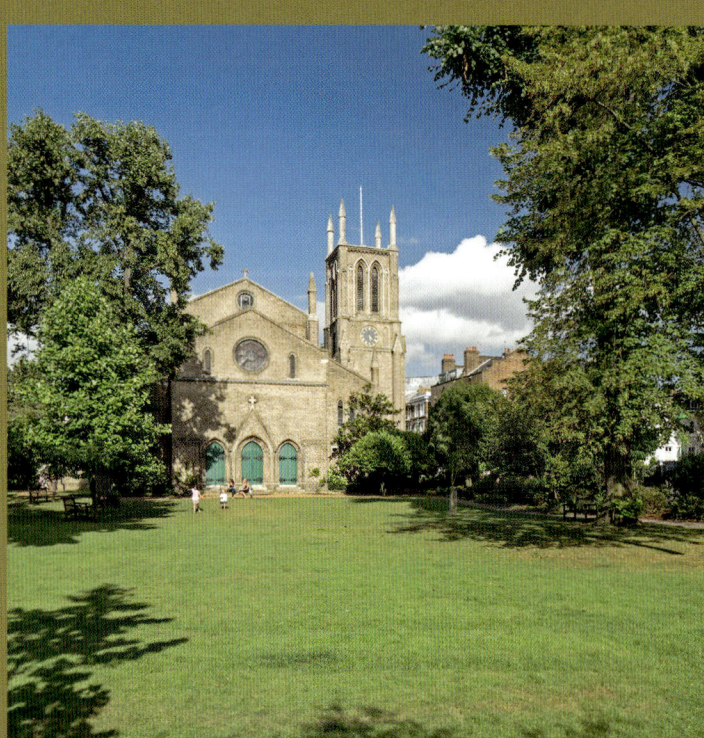

St James's Gardens

Laid out in an informal woodland style, the garden is dominated by mature chestnut and lime trees some of which date back to when the garden was established in the mid nineteenth century. The garden continues to be maintained by residents of the surrounding square.

The garden is dominated by Lewis Vulliamy's church of St. James Norland which was consecrated in 1845, unfortunately without a spire due to lack of funds. It made marketing history last century when £150,000 was raised towards restoration costs from a single mail-shot – 90% of the donors never having previously given to the church.

Thank you to Amanda and Martin Frame for allowing
me to take these pictures throughout the past year.

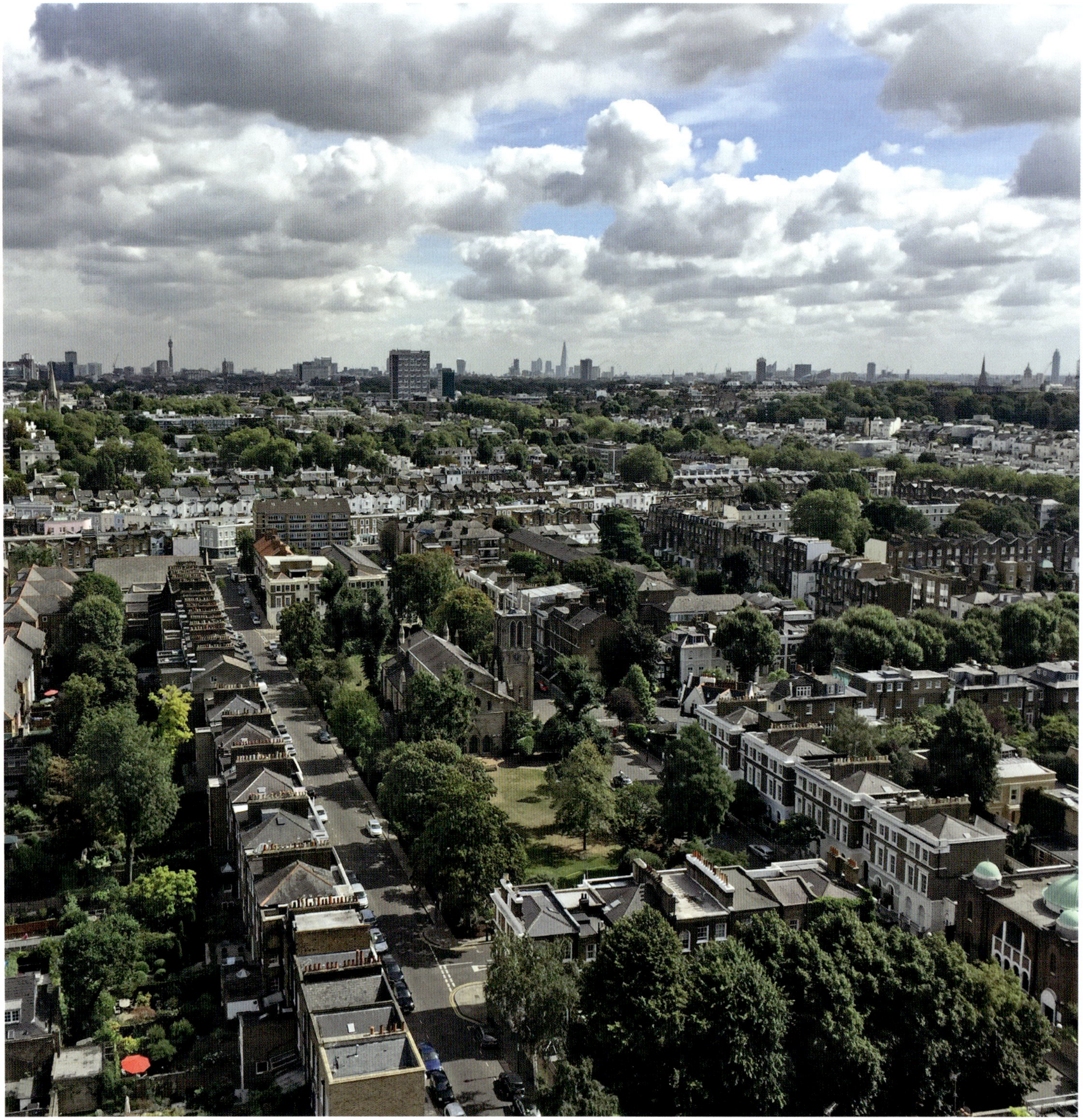

Thank you to Angela Baptiste, a resident at the top of Poynter Tower, off St Anne's Villas, for allowing me to take the picture opposite and on pages 6 and 7 from her flat.

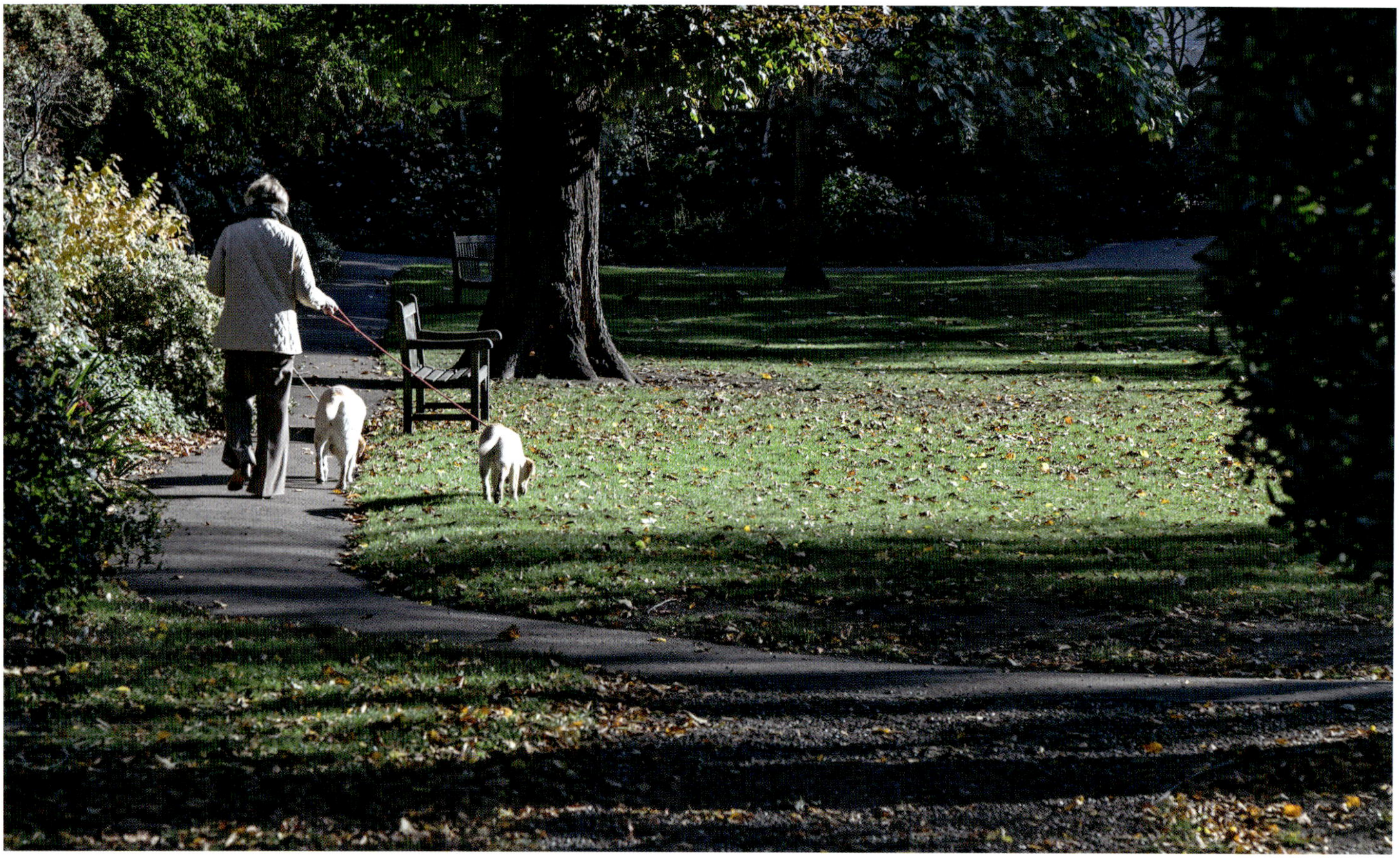

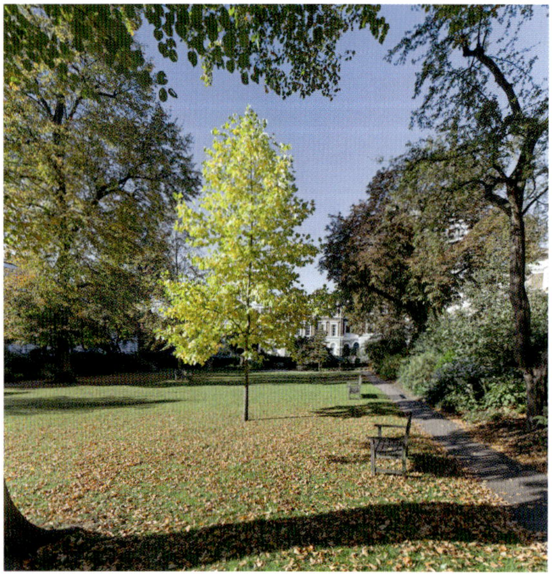

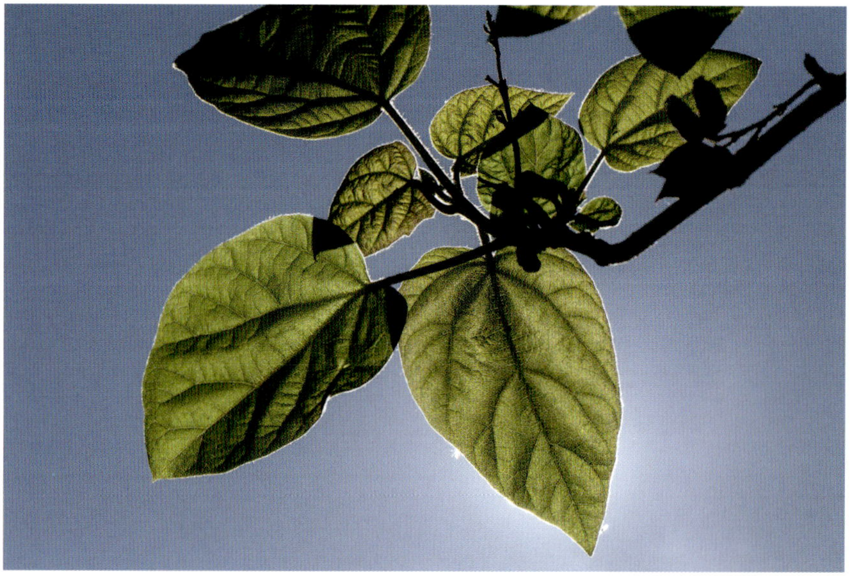

Opposite bottom right: Catalpa

Top: Magnolia

Bottom left: Hydrangea

Bottom right: African Lily

Holland Park Avenue

The road is so named as it ran through grounds formerly belonging to nearby Jacobean Holland House.

Opposite top: With grand houses guarded by lines of statuesque plane trees, Holland Park Avenue feels more like a European boulevard than a major traffic route.

Opposite bottom: Located toward the bottom end of Holland Park Avenue, Norland Place School was established in 1876 and counts George Osborne and Rosalind Franklin among its many distinguished alumni.

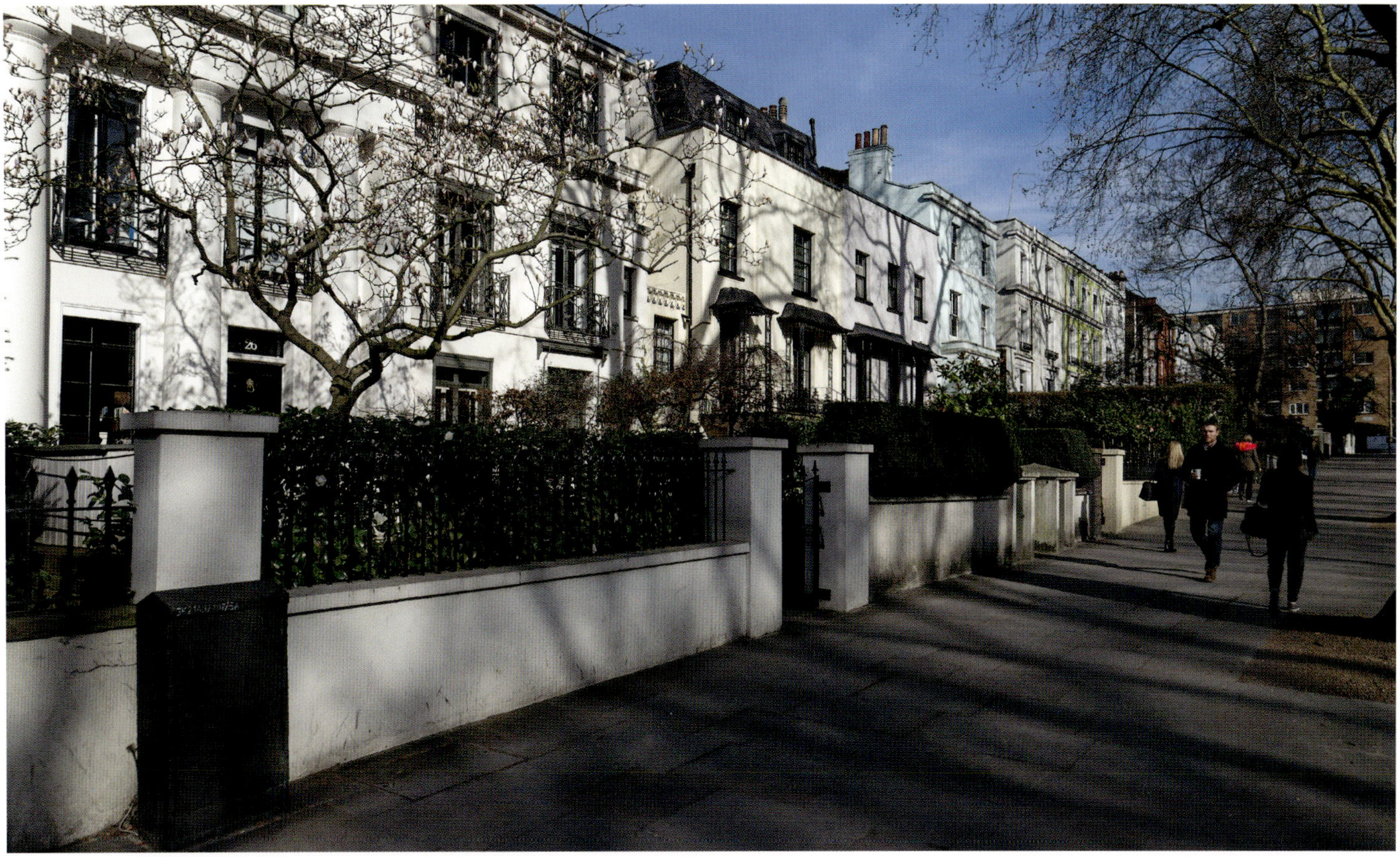

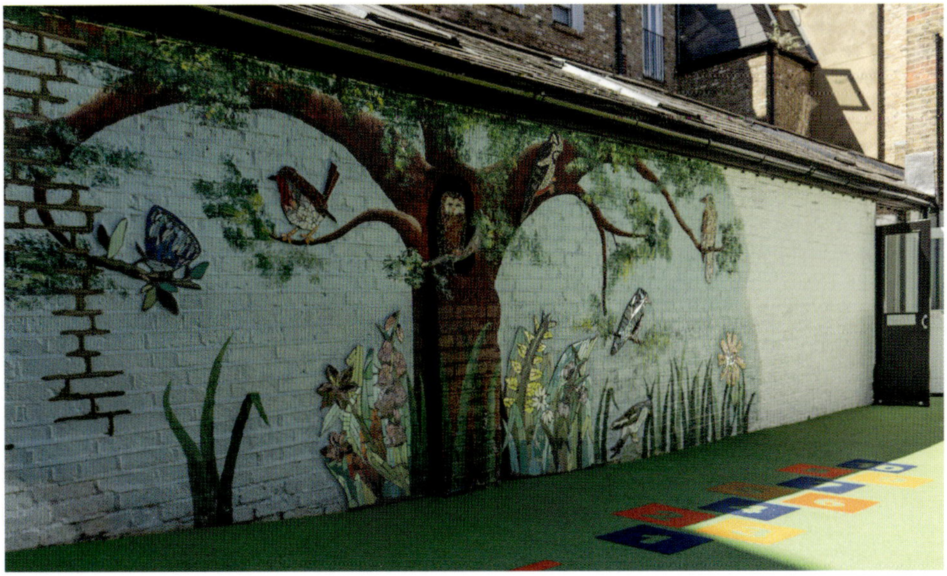

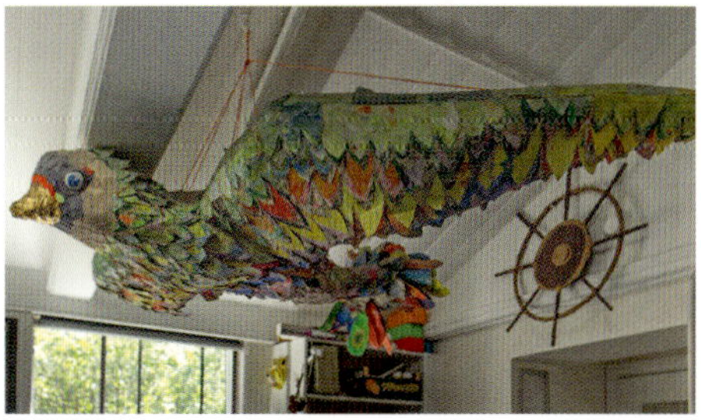

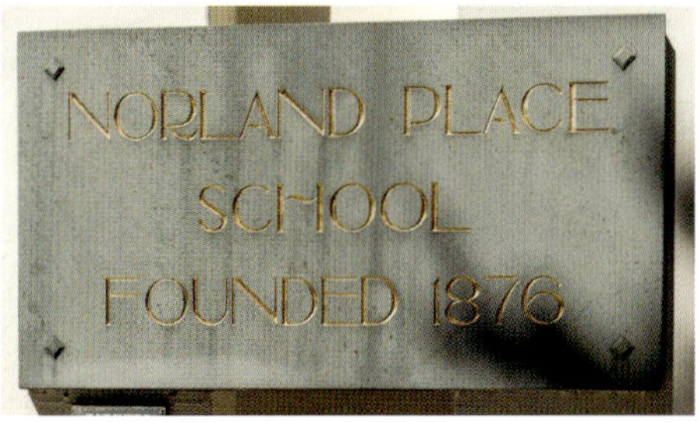
NORLAND PLACE
SCHOOL
FOUNDED 1876

Bottom left: Danny Lidgate is the fifth generation of his family to run their butcher's shop on Holland Park Avenue.

Bottom right: Daunts Bookshop always has an interesting window at Christmas time.

This page: Ladbroke Grove as seen from Holland Park Avenue. It was James Weller Ladbroke who planned a spectacular estate focused on a central circus leading off a broad avenue. The avenue was named Ladbroke Grove and is a reminder today of his vision.

Inset: The same scene as pictured early last century.

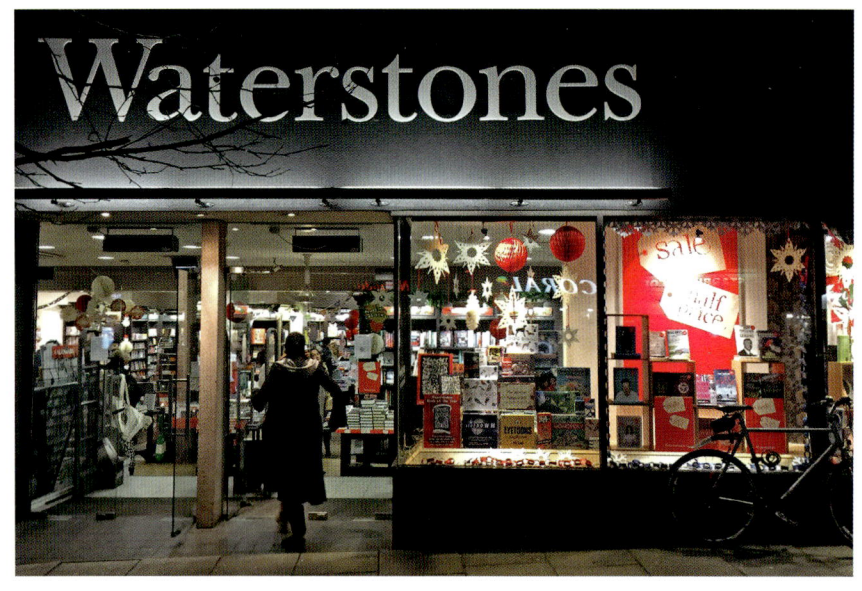

Right: Built at the cost of £25,000 the splendid Coronet was described as a 'theatre of which the whole country may be proud' when it opened in 1898. With seating for more than a thousand, a crush bar, huge proscenium arch, curved balcony and red velvet seats as well as six gilt boxes upholstered in red plush it certainly was a spectacular venue to watch famous thespians including Sir Henry Irving and Mrs. Patrick Campbell. But eventually the stage gave way to talking pictures and despite several closure threats over the years, it continues to entertain cinema audiences. There is also a resident ghost which is most active around Christmas week, the anniversary when a cashier threw herself off the balcony in the early 1900s having been found with her fingers in the till.

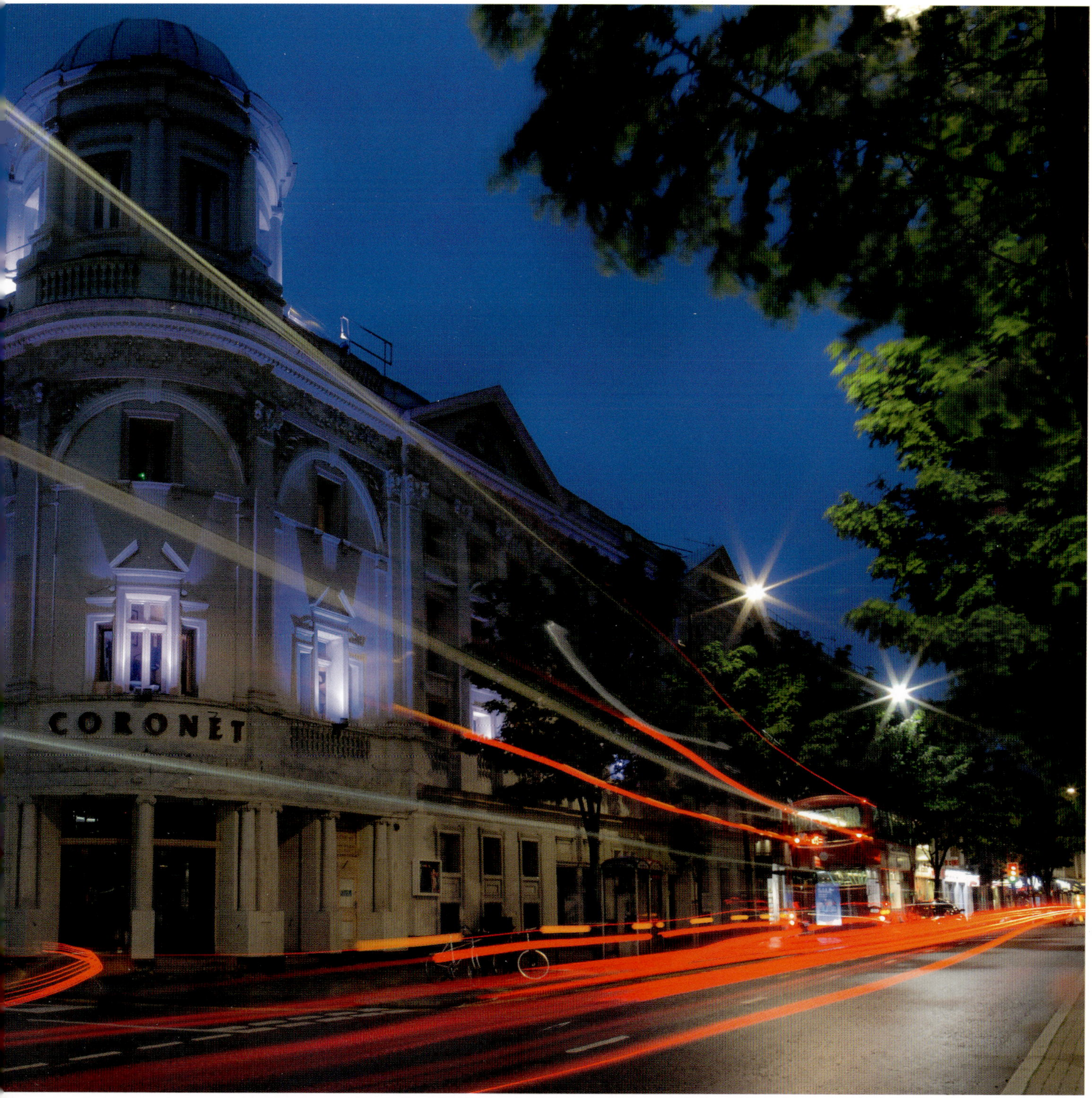
CORONET

Top right: Hellebore

Royal Crescent Garden

These gardens are part of the Norland Estate and were developed by Robert Cantwell who laid out Royal Crescent in 1846.

The original paths have been simplified and a specially designed gazebo surrounded by a rose and lavender bed replaces the original central fountain feature. Many of the magnificent trees date back to when the garden was originally laid out though two plane trees may well be even older.

In recent years the garden committee has worked with a garden designer to upgrade the design, enhance the planting perimeter beds and replace old and dying trees and shrubs which has resulted in the garden winning several awards:

Second prize in the Garden Squares North category of the Brighter Kensington & Chelsea Scheme; and a silver certificate in the Private Squares Large category of the London Squares Garden Competition run by the London Gardens Society.

Thank you to Helen Murlis, who has just retired from leading the garden committee, for allowing me to take these pictures throughout the past year.

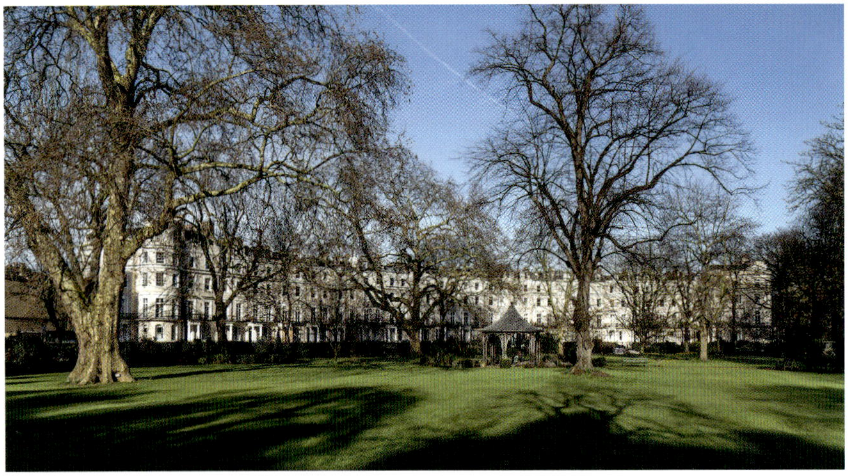

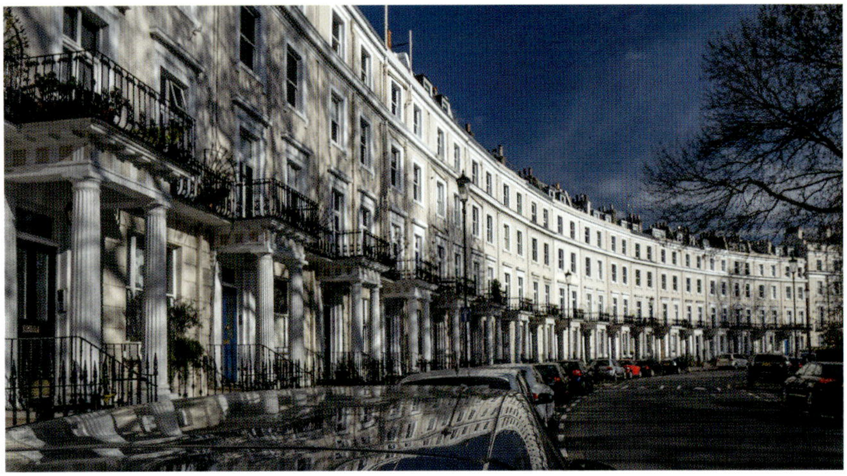

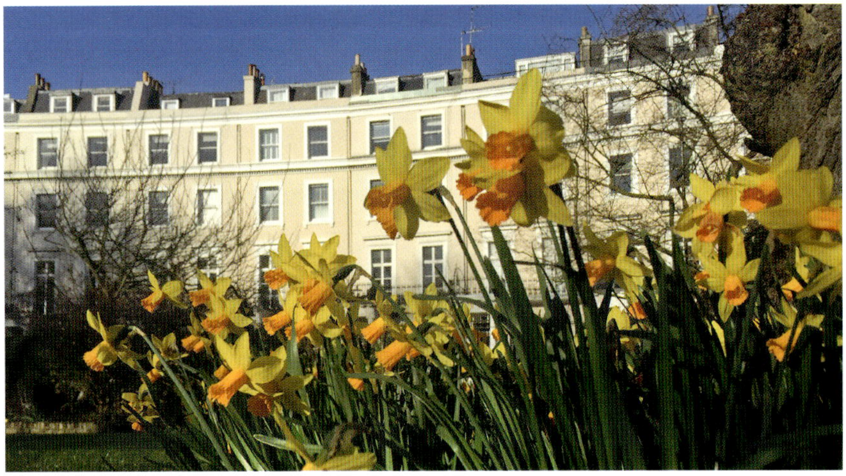

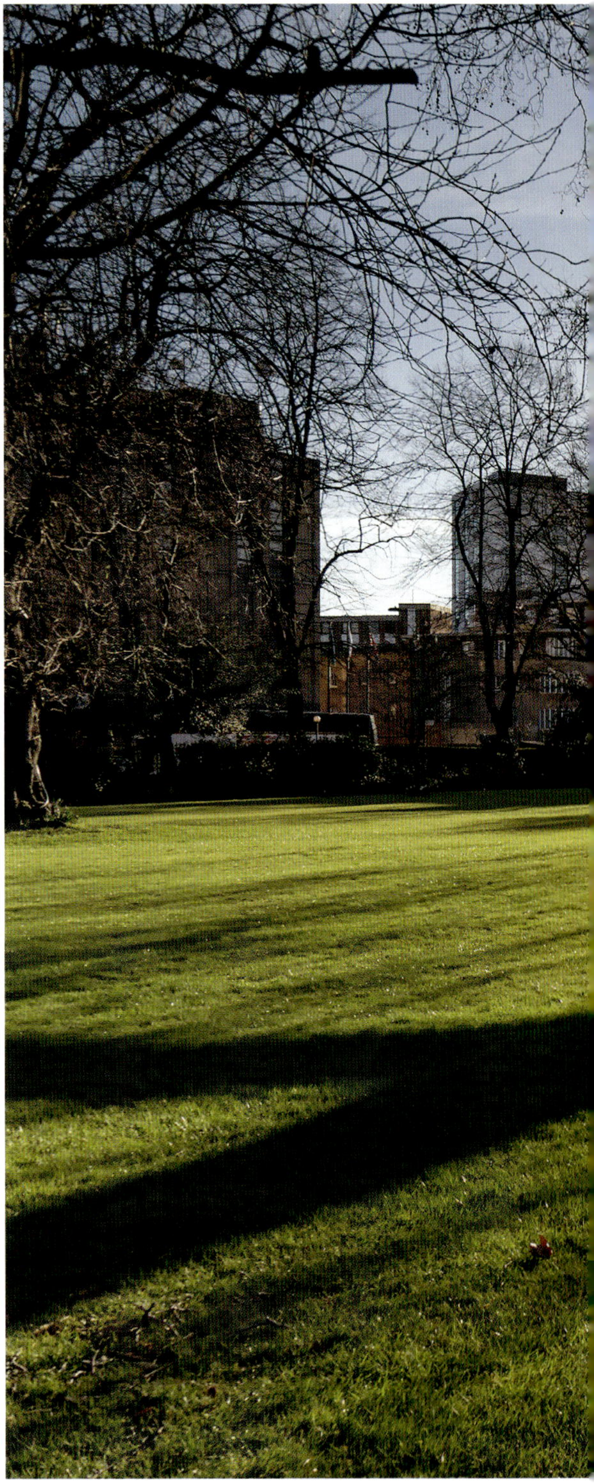

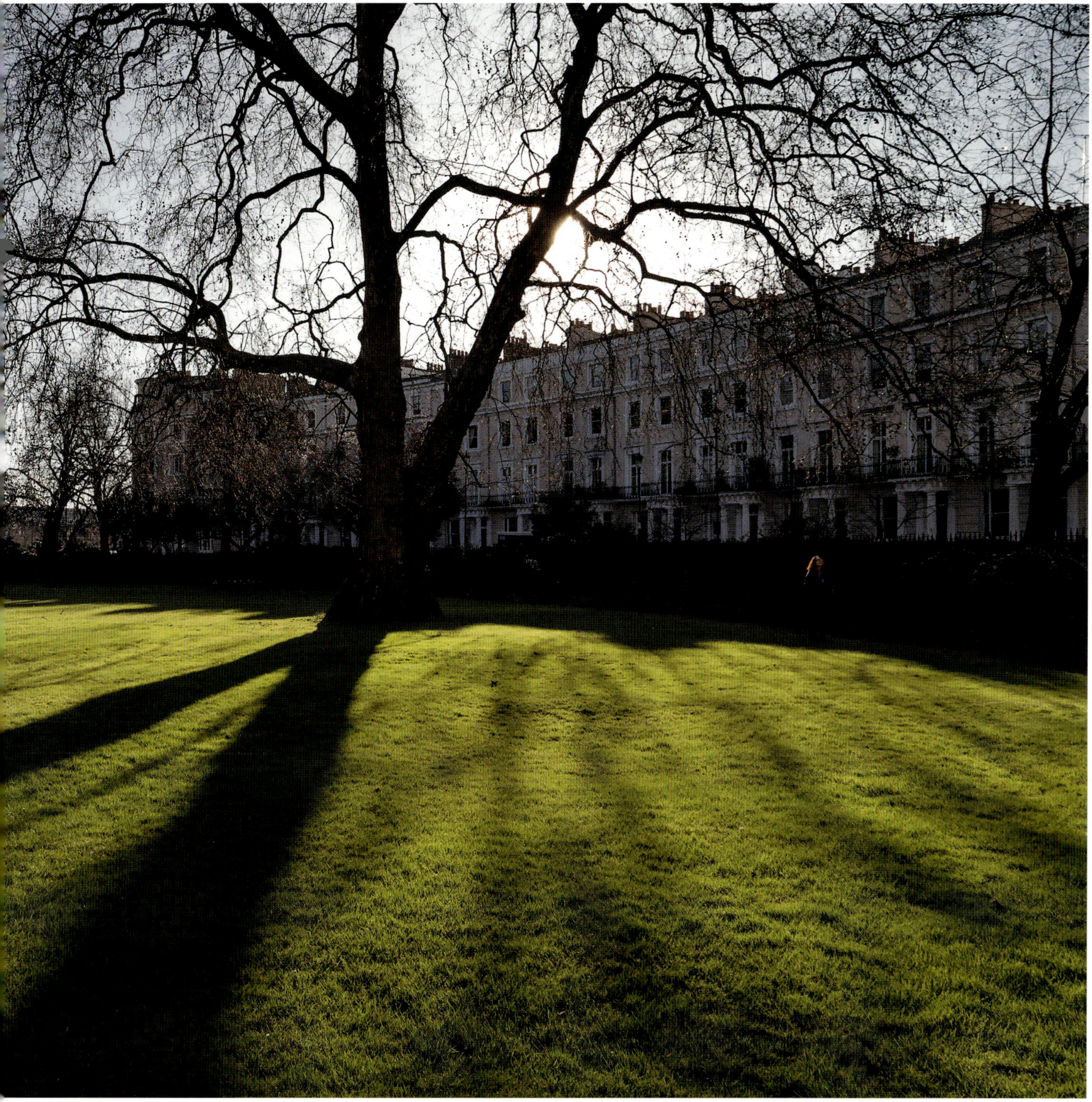

Bottom right: Pink rose

Above: Chrysanthemum

Norland Square

The Norland estate spread over fifty-two acres with the house standing near the site of today's 130 Holland Park Avenue. The house burned down in 1825 and shortly after the remaining land was developed for housing including the imposing Royal Crescent and delightful Norland Square.

Thank you to Lana from the garden committee, for allowing me to take the pictures inside the garden during Open Garden Squares weekend back in June.

Norland Nannies with their distinct brown uniform are the crème-de-la-crème of nannies. The Training School for Ladies as Children's Nurses was founded in 1892 by Emily Ward and soon became known as the Norland Institute due to its location in Norland Place (opposite). For many years it occupied larger premises in Pembridge Square before moving to Bath in 2003.

119

A walk around east Notting Hill

TIME: APPROX. 1 HOUR 15 MINUTES

If you arrive by tube at Notting Hill take exit 3 signposted "Portobello Road and Market" which brings you on to the north side of Notting Hill Gate. Across the road is the Gate Cinema which has undergone several transformations since opening in 1861 as the North End and Harvey Dining Room – it has been a hotel, coffee palace and even a brothel, finally being converted to an electric cinema in 1911 and whilst today's exterior is of little merit, the interior retains much of it's Edwardian plaster-work. Next door is the magnificent Coronet which opened as a theatre in 1898 with Ellen Terry and Sarah Bernhardt treading the boards but succumbed to moving pictures some twenty years later. Turn right into Pembridge Road (1 and 2) where until 1864 there was a turnpike gate with a charge of three pence to take your horse and cart through. Continue straight ahead but look at number 32 as you pass, The Victoria Wine Company was here in 1865.

Turn left into Portobello Road where the Sun in Splendour pub (3) with its curving yellow frontage has been serving customers since the 1850s. Originally called Green Lane and leading to a farm, when the farm was renamed in honour of the great naval victory at Puerto Bello in the Gulf of Mexico in 1739 so the lane changed it's name too. The oldest cottages are on the right and number 22 has a plaque to George Orwell who once lived there, cross Chepstow Villas and glance up to the left at the advertisement

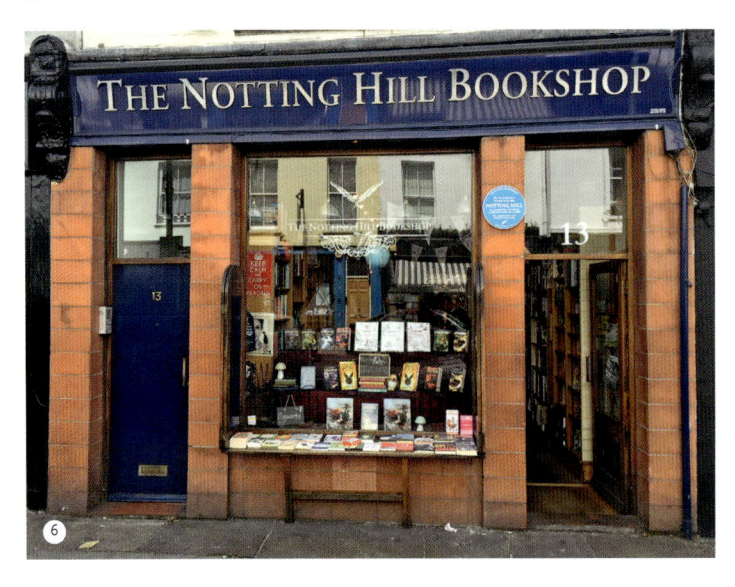

A. Davey Builder put on the wall in 1851. The market (4) starts here and in 1870 was regarded as 'the market centre of Kensington' and since the bric-a-brac vendors arrived this first part has given way to antique traders and claims to be the largest antique market in the world. Cross Westbourne Grove and the blue plaque over number 115 records that June Aylward established the first antique shop here, another blue plaque at 169 is for Susan Garth who opened the first antique market. The old shop sign at 175 to former local butcher G. Portwine is a reminder of the now long gone independent bakers, greengrocers and fishmongers who once traded here. After Elgin Crescent the street stalls are piled high with a wide range of fruit and vegetables whilst cheerful costermongers loudly call out to attract customers. The Electric Cinema (5) has been here since 1911 and is one of the oldest working cinemas in the country, unfortunately the underground public toilets with their elegant railings at Talbot Road have long since closed so continue onwards past the Salvation Army Citadel and turn left into Westbourne Park Road. Number 280 is the actual blue door used in the film of *Notting Hill* which was magically relocated to Portobello Road, whilst just a few doors away there is a house displaying an amusing mural.

At Kensington Park Road turn left, the modern housing development of Convent Garden across the way is a reminder that a hundred years ago the Dominican nuns had their home in the vicinity. The local Jewish community has also moved away and their synagogue at number 206 closed in 2000, just a hundred years after it was built. To your left 13 Blenheim Crescent has a plaque about the famous Notting Hill Bookshop (6), continue down Kensington Park Road and past Notting Hill Community Church (7) which started life in 1862 as the Peniel Chapel. You are now walking through the Ladbroke Estate and splendid Kensington Park Terrace North built around 1853 overlooks leafy gardens opposite which are firmly locked as they are for the sole use of the residents whose houses back on to them. Cross Westbourne Grove and the Notting Hill Kitchen (8) with its charming blue tiles is where Prue Leith opened her first restaurant in 1969, next door is the church dedicated to St. Peter with its imposing Corinthian columns and splendid domed tower. Ladbroke Square, the last enclosed garden on this walk, is one of the largest private communal squares in London and the original Gardener's Cottage looks across the road at the blocks of red-brick mansion flats which were built in the 1930s after the demolition of several gracious Victorian villas.

Horbury Crescent (9) on your right (please note the coal hole covers in the Crescent, which are typical of the area) takes you into Ladbroke Road where to the left there are two blue plaques fixed to the hall of the former Horbury Chapel. It was here that

Ashley Dukes opened the Mercury Theatre in 1931 and his wife Marie Rambert found a home for her newly formed ballet company. The main chapel building built in 1848 is now known as Kensington Temple and home to the Elim Pentecostal Church. The green shelter (10) in the middle of the road is a listed building and was built in 1909 by the Cabmen's Shelter Fund to provide a place for cabmen to obtain 'good and wholesome refreshments at moderate prices' and thereby keep them out of the pub. The shops on the road's bend have resisted several threats of demolition over the years and the walk finishes at the Prince Albert which has been here since the 1840s and conveniently at one time had a brewery next door. It is also home to The Gate Theatre, founded in 1979 and known for specialising in international productions.

Walk devised by Caroline MacMillan
www.westlondonwalks.co.uk

Wesley Square

The delightful award winning garden of Wesley Square was designed as a haven of peace and beauty for the surrounding modern dwellings.

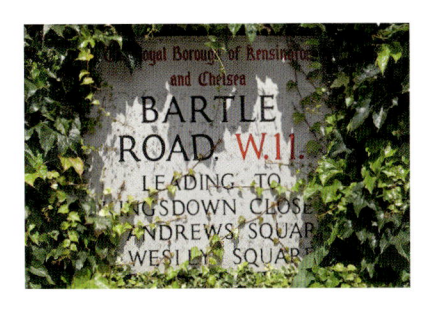

Top right: You will not find Rillington Place (just off Wesley Square) marked on any maps of London. Number 10 was the home of notorious murderer John Christie who in the mid twentieth century murdered up to eight people, including his wife, who he buried in the house and garden. The entire street was eventually demolished and Bartle Road now occupies the area, though a house was never built on the site of number 10 Rillington Place.

Thank you to Hilary Arnold, their head gardener, who kindly let me take these pictures during Open Garden Squares weekend.

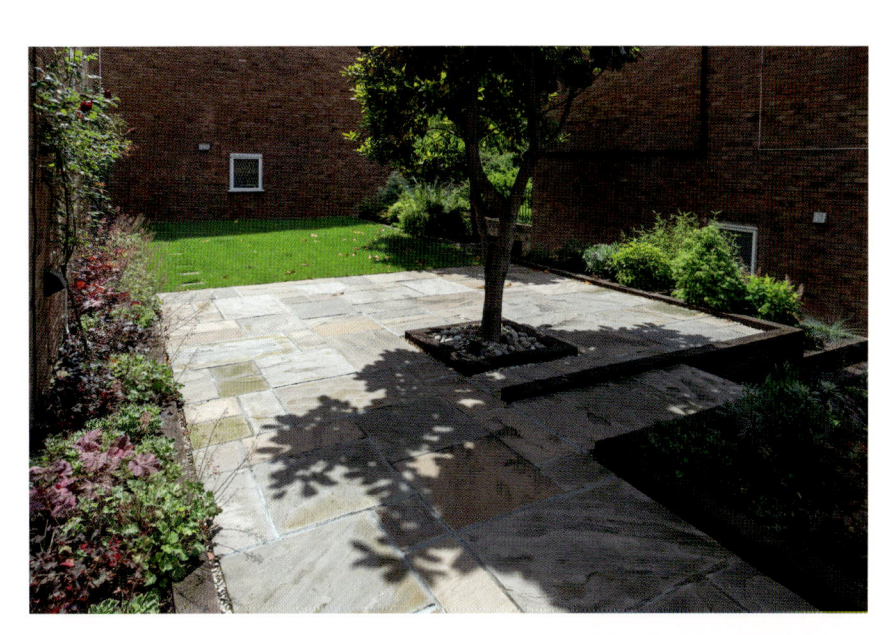

Lancaster Green

This page: Kensington Aldridge Academy

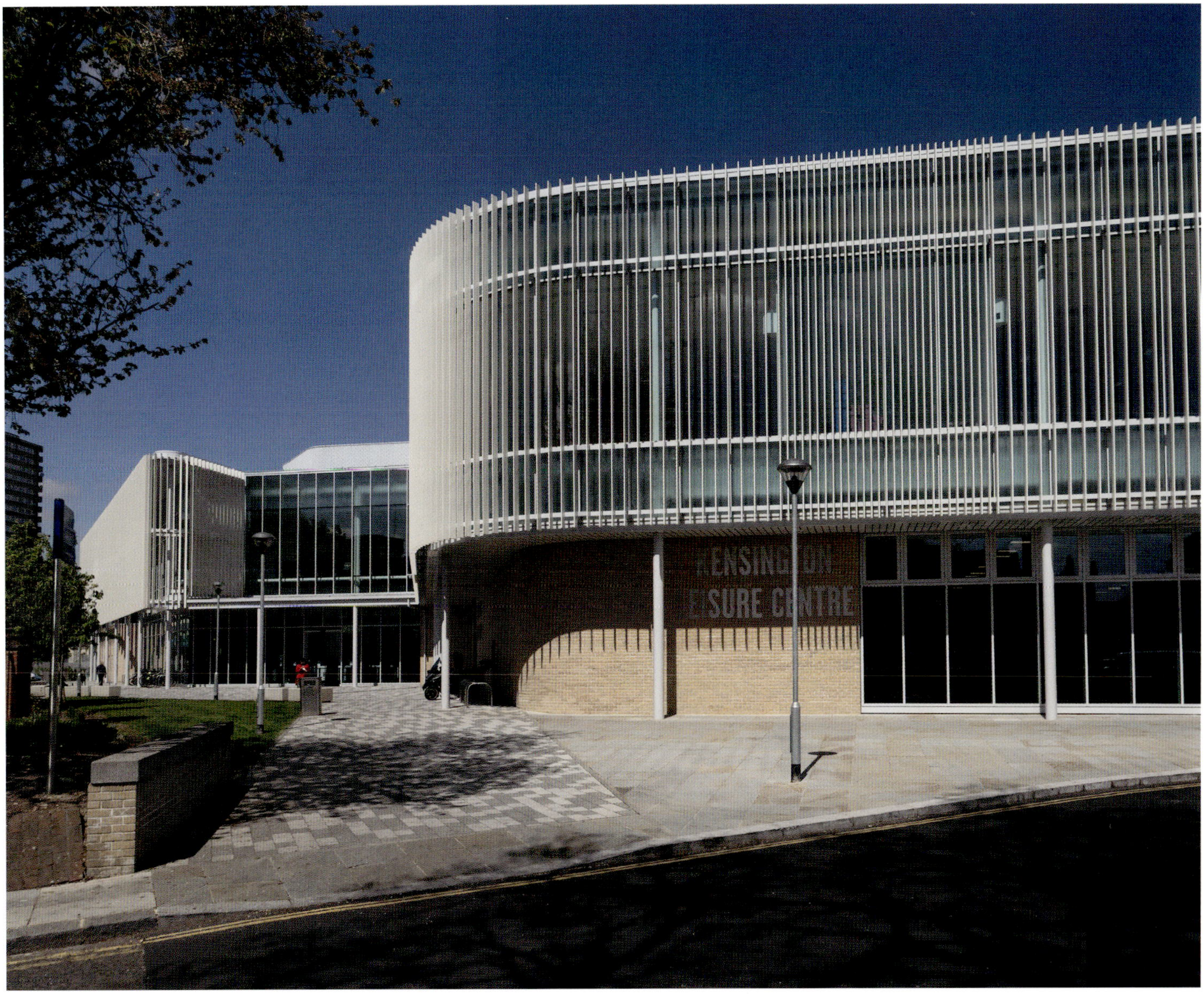

This page: Lancaster Road

In the Beatles' film *A Hard Day's Night*, Ringo Starr is seen being chased down Lancaster Road.

128

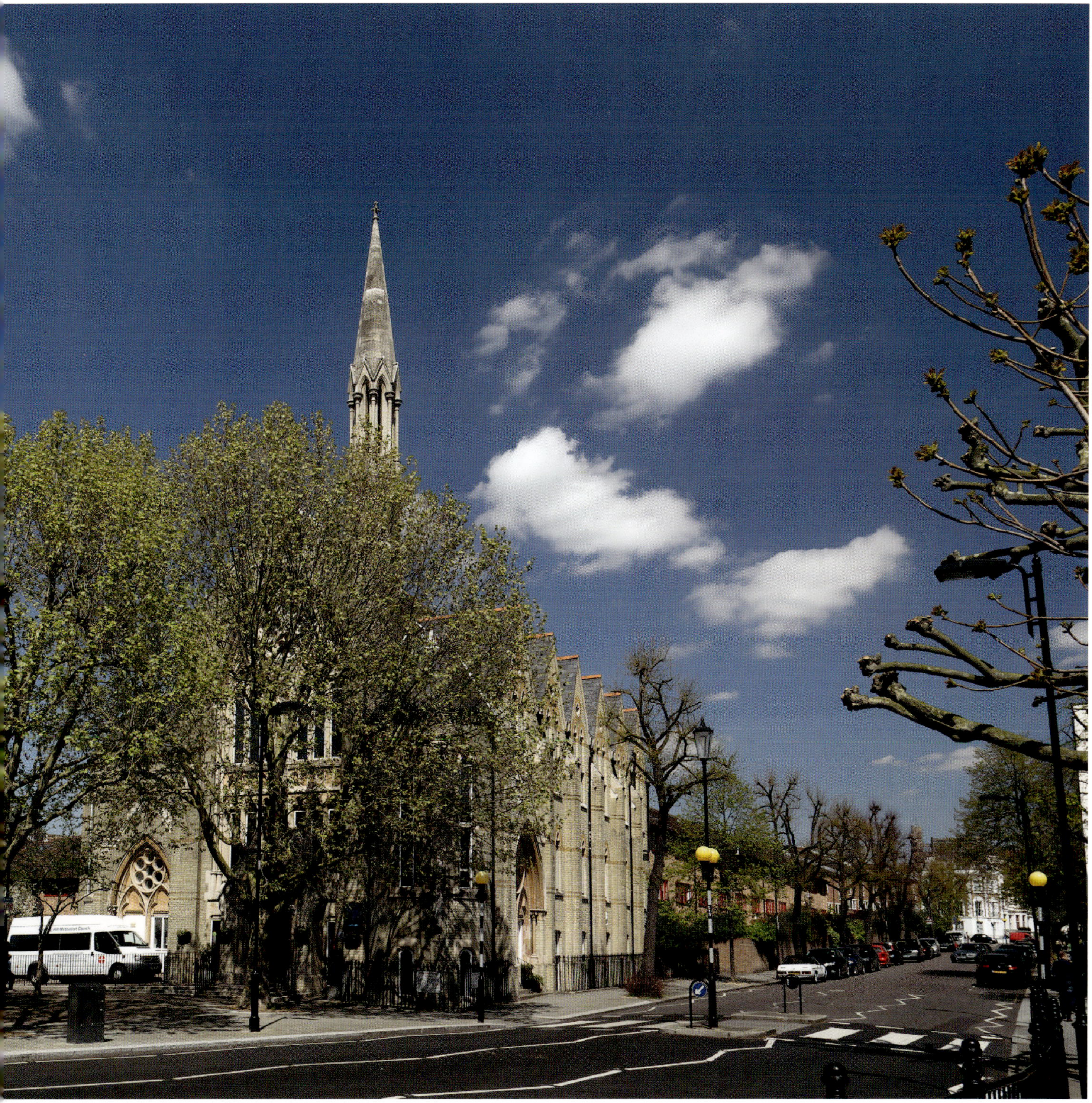

Frestonia

In the early 1970s squatters occupied some of the semi-derelict properties around Latimer Road including Freston and Bramley Roads. Inspired by the Ealing comedy film *Passport to Pimlico* the group declared the area independent of the UK and so the Free and Independent Republic of Frestonia was created.

Passports were issued, postage stamps printed which the Post Office honoured and an application for membership sent to the United Nations.

Left: It is no longer possible to sip a pint at the bar of the Bramley Arms as it closed as a pub in the 1980s, but you can see it on screen as it was used as a location for the films *The Lavender Hill Mob* and *Quadrophenia*.

Top right: The People's Hall has certainly led an interesting life since it was built in 1901. It became the focal meeting place for the residents of newly formed Frestonia who gathered there to watch the film *Passport to Pimlico* and The Clash used the recording studios for their album *Combat Rock*.

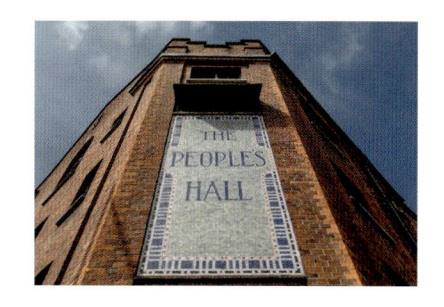

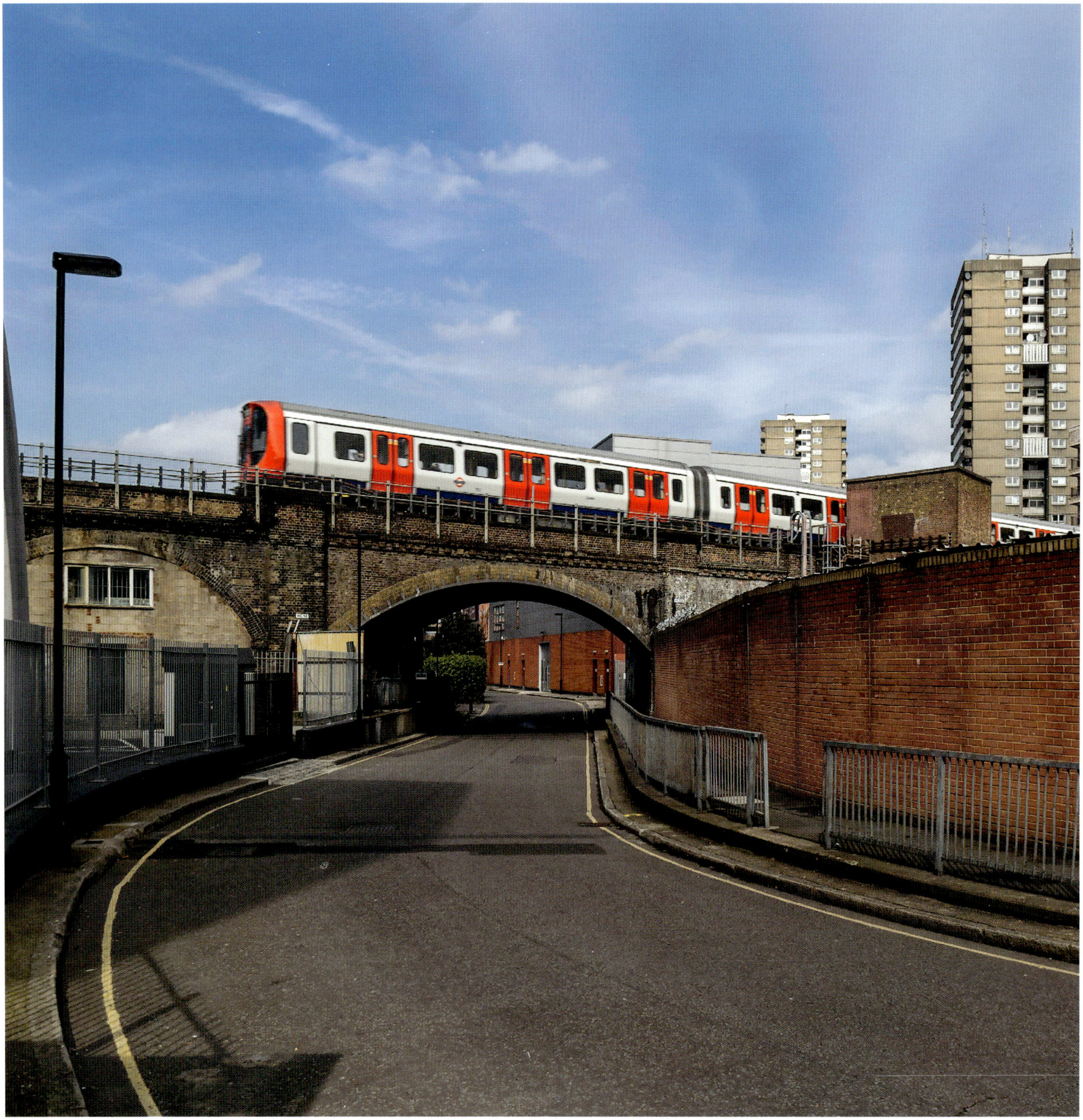

Bottom left: Latimer Road Station was nicknamed Piggery Junction when it opened in 1868 due to its proximity to the slum area known as The Piggeries.

Opposite: Bard Road

Avondale Park

Avondale Park was created in 1892 during a general redevelopment of the area which had declined due to the establishment of nearby piggeries and potteries.

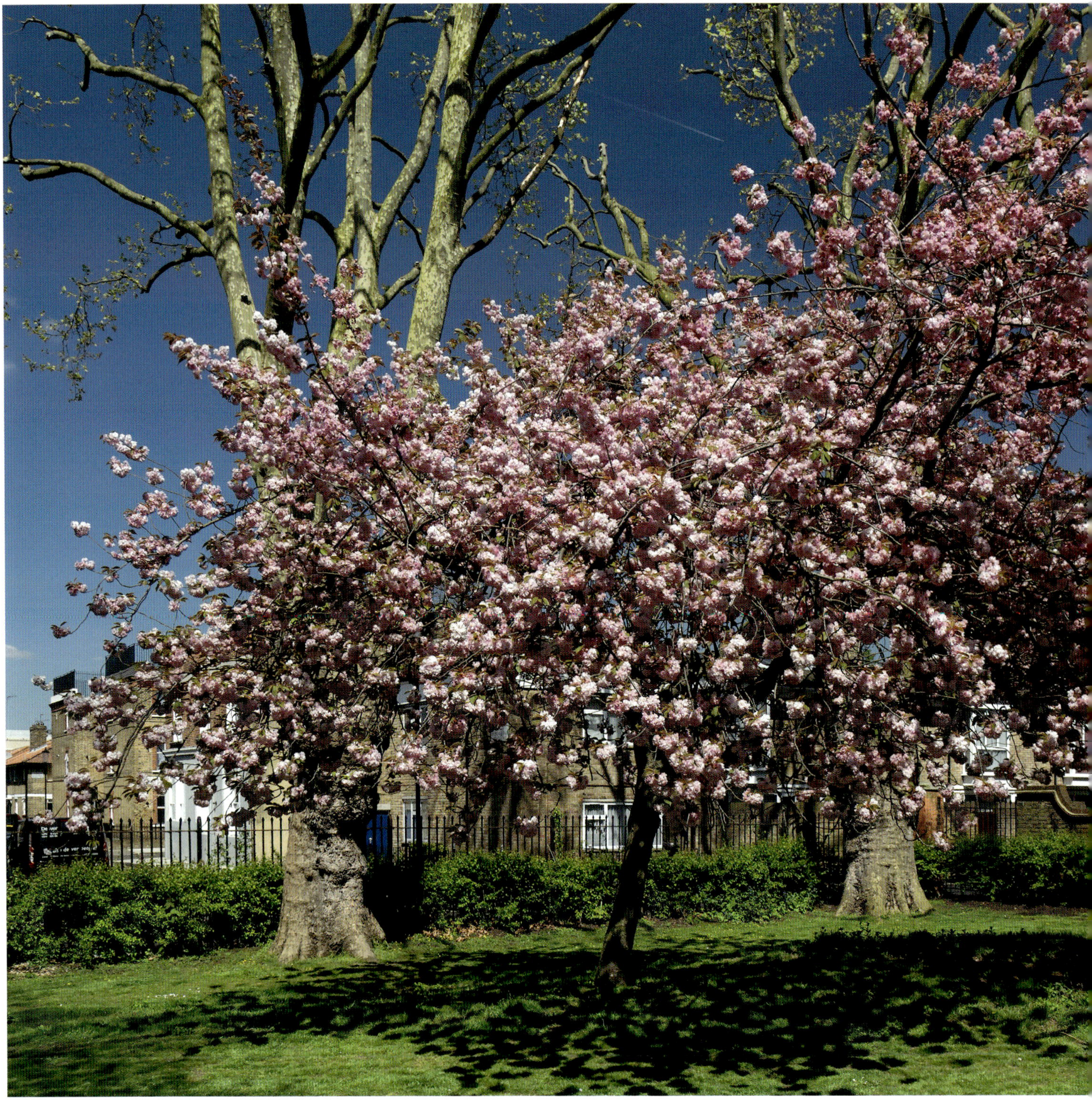

The park has a grass free lawn made entirely from 65 different species of flowers which form a patchwork of colour and scent throughout the year.

138

This page: In the 1880s the school, then known as St. Clement's Road School, was nicknamed "The Penny Board" and it was said that children were bribed there by the gift of sweets.

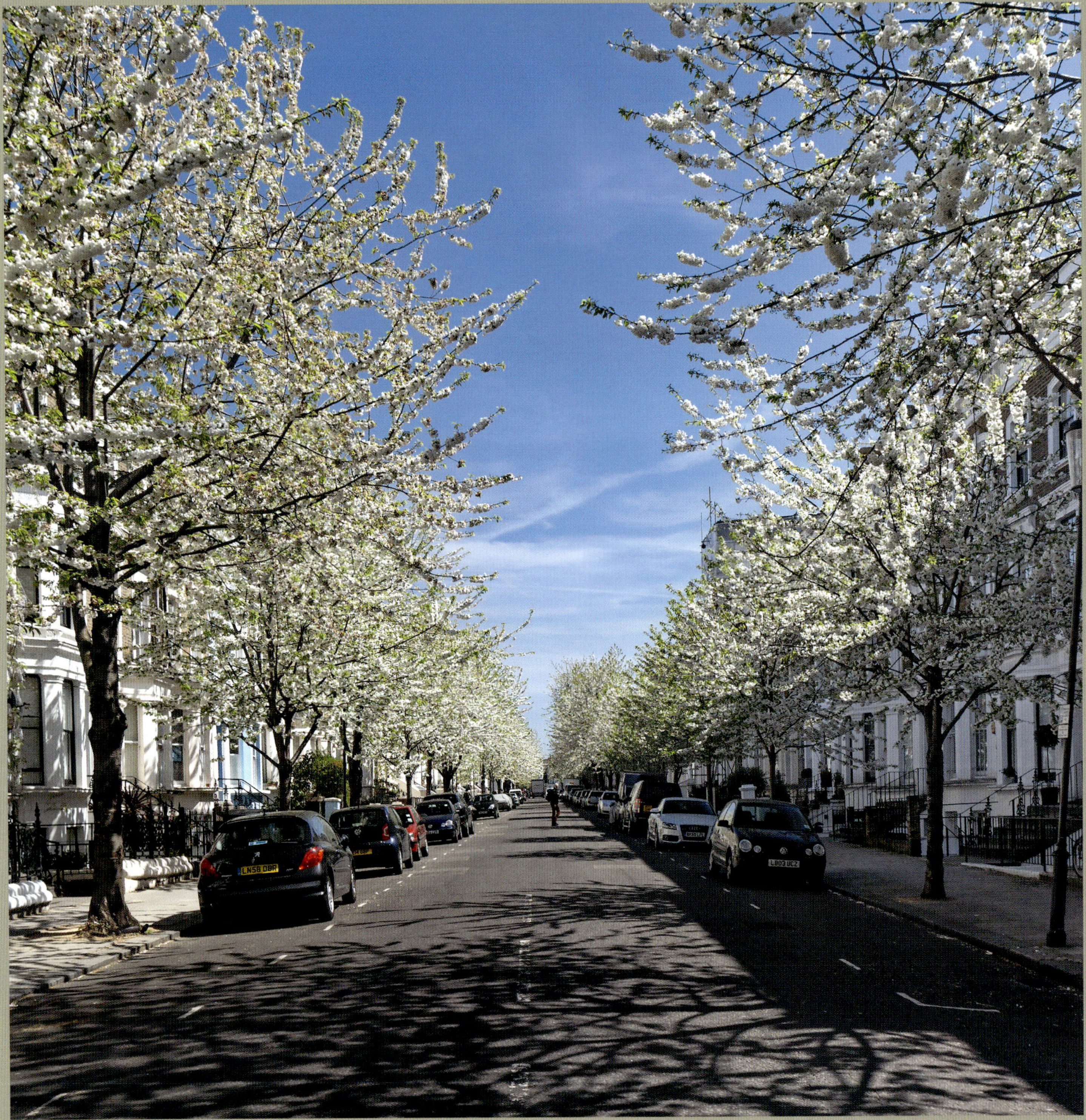

North Kensington

Following the successful development of nearby Kensal Green, Kensal New Town was laid out in the 1840s on 140 acres of land belonging to the parish of St. Luke in Chelsea. But the fortune of the area deteriorated due to a lack of employment and chronic overcrowding, and sandwiched between the canal and main railway line in to Paddington Station this detached part of North Kensington earned the nick-name Chelsea-in-the-Wilderness. In recent times a multicultural community including residents of Afro-Caribbean, Portuguese and Moroccan birth or descent has established itself here and the area is once again undergoing redevelopment.

Opposite: the spectacular display of blossom on Chesterton Road.

St. Charles Hospital

Below: It was in 1881 that the St. Marylebone Union Infirmary opened in St. Charles Square to treat the sick poor of Marylebone. A few years later Florence Nightingale established a training school for nurses at the infirmary. When the LCC took over administrative charge it was renamed St. Charles Hospital and subsequently became part of the NHS, the building is now Grade II listed.

Bottom left and right: The Earl of Shrewsbury and Talbot built his imposing 1903 headquarters in Barlby Road as a showroom and factory for the popular French Clement cars he was importing to Britain. The brick workshops were built to the highest standard and equipped with the most modern of machine tools whilst the reception area resembled a miniature palace complete with marble Ionic columns, frescoes and stained glass windows.

Pall Mall Deposit was the first depository to be built using reinforced concrete. Since opening in 1911 it has stored millions of items including household furniture and personal effects and in 1991 was converted into offices, workshops and recording studios.

A former print works in Barlby Road has been transformed into luxurious apartments and appropriately called The Ink Building.

Top and bottom left: In the 1930s Rootes Motors took over the Clement Talbot factory in Barlby Road. Eventually the land was developed for housing and Sunbeam Crescent, Hillman and Humber Drives are reminders on the Rootes Estate of the cars once manufactured here.

Below: Established in 1903 as part of the vision of the development of the St. Quintin Estate to provide sports and recreation for residents, the West London Bowling Club hidden off Quintin Avenue is one of the secret delights of W10. Over the years it has produced champion bowlers and the award winning gardens together with green and clubhouse are maintained through the voluntary efforts of its members.

Little Wormwood Scrubs

The West London Railway opened a line in 1844 connecting Kensington (via Shepherd's Bush) with Wormwood Scrubs and so linked in to the main line running between London and Birmingham. By crossing the common it carved a section off, which became Little Wormwood Scrubs.

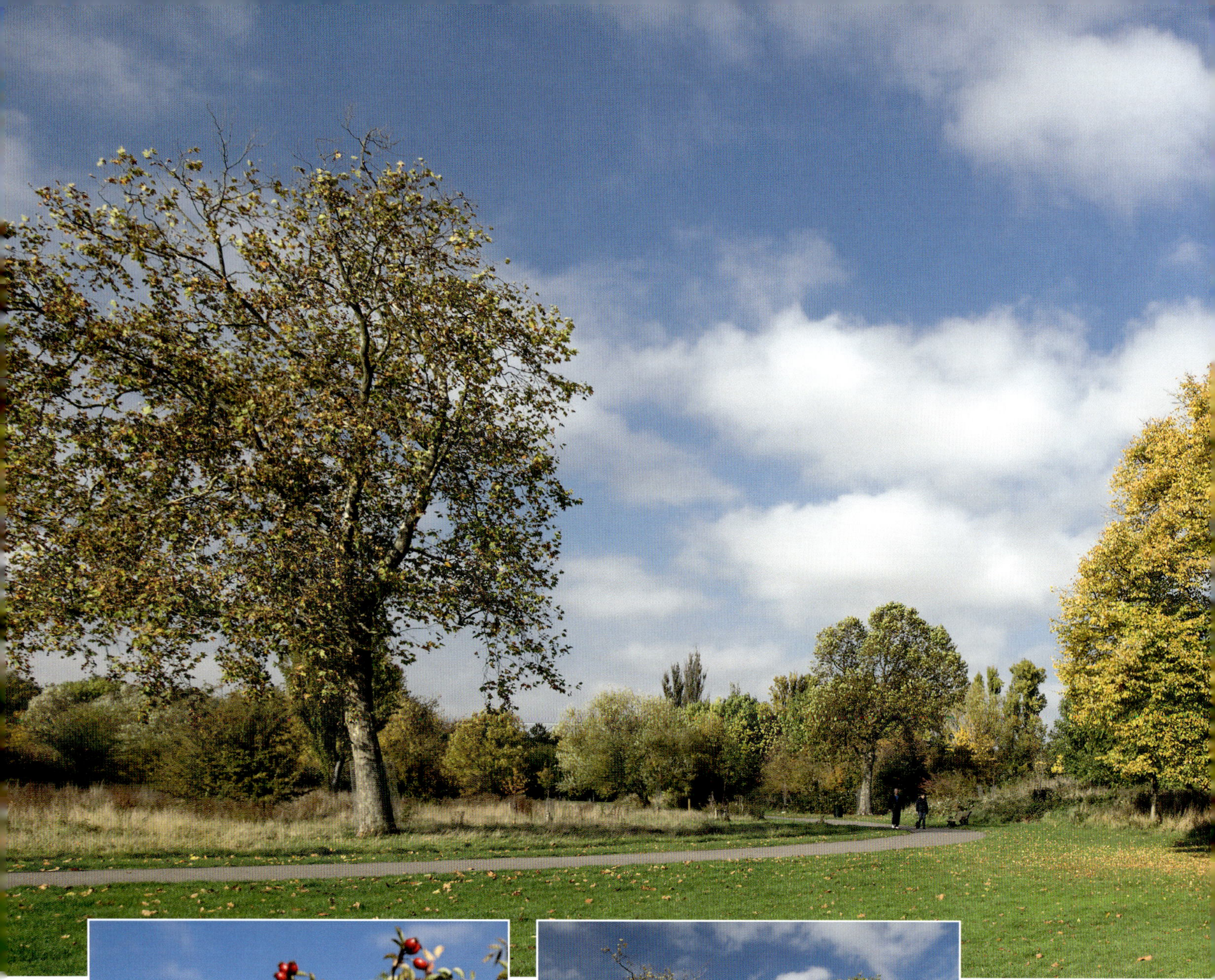
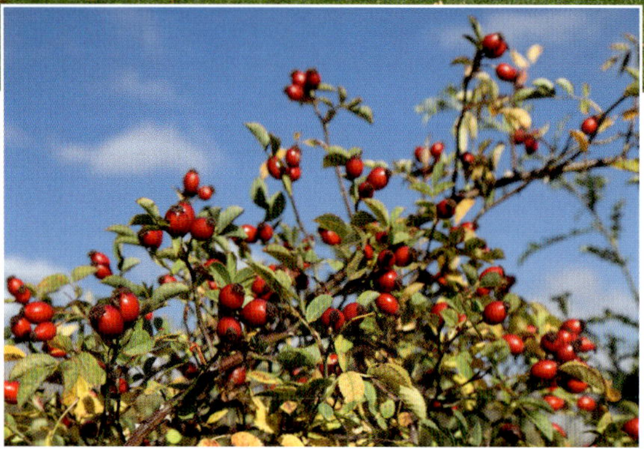
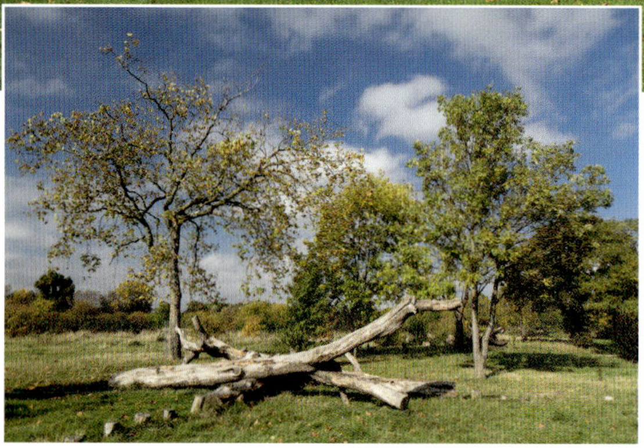

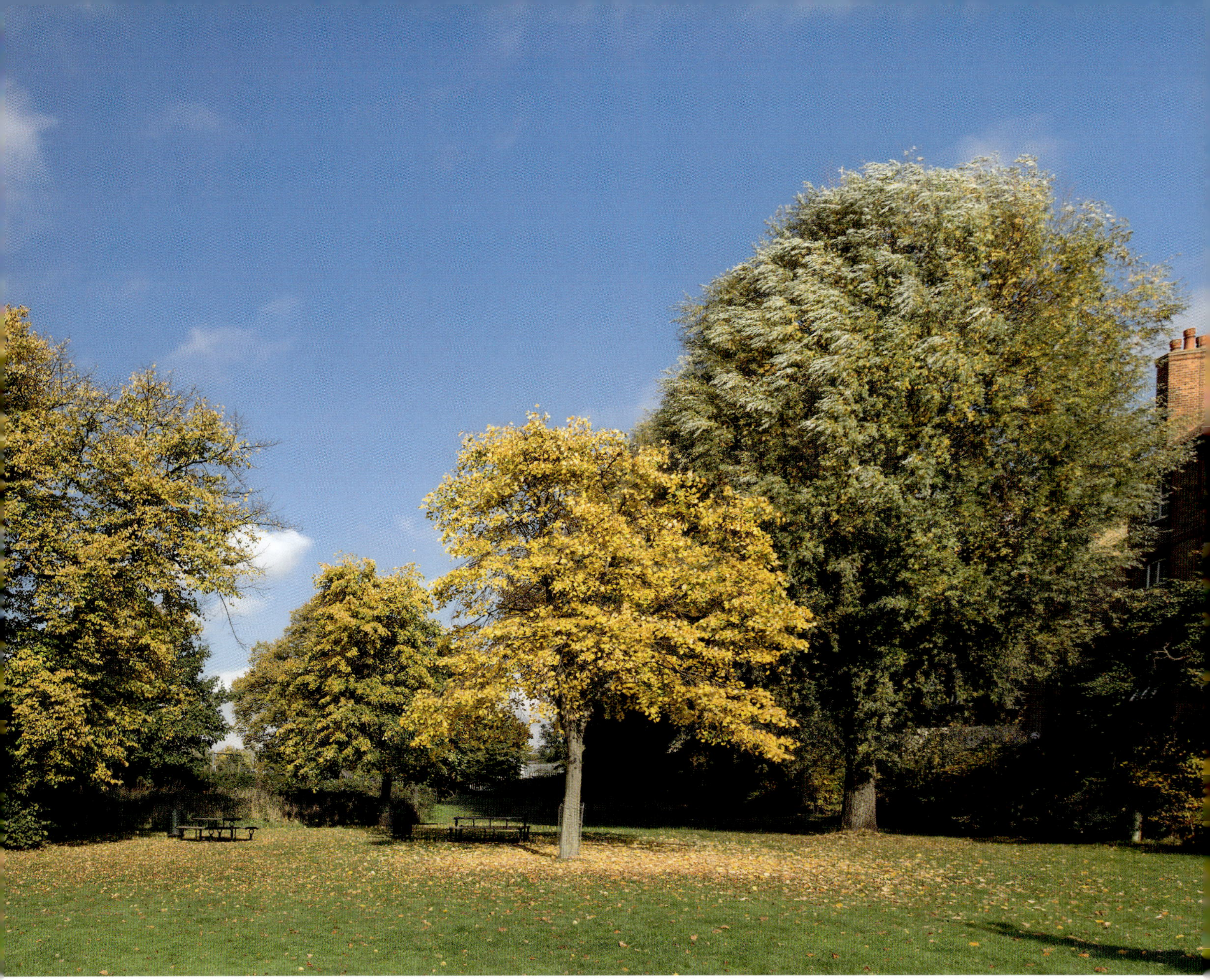

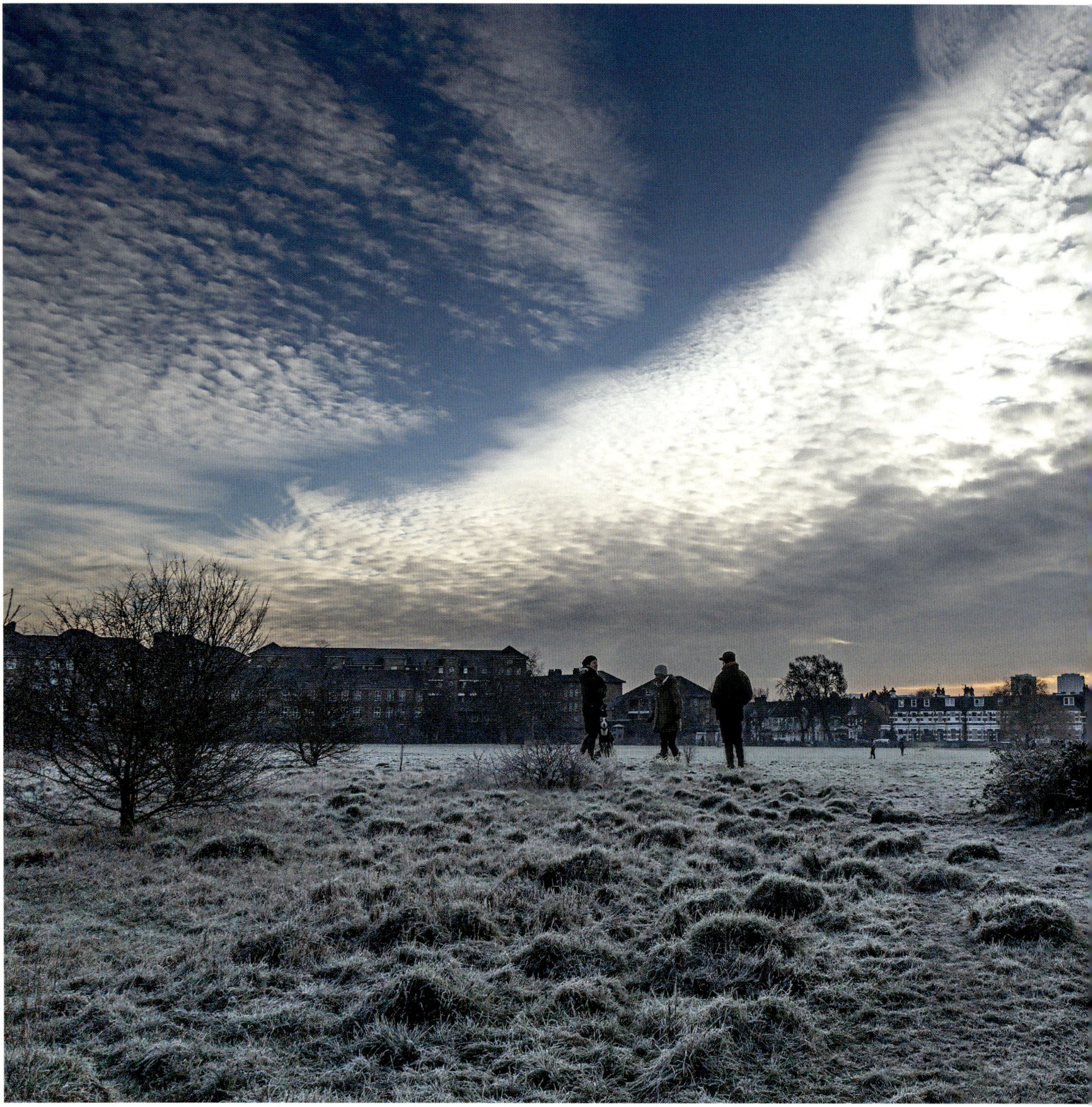

153

A walk around North Kensington

TIME: 1 HOUR 15 MINUTES

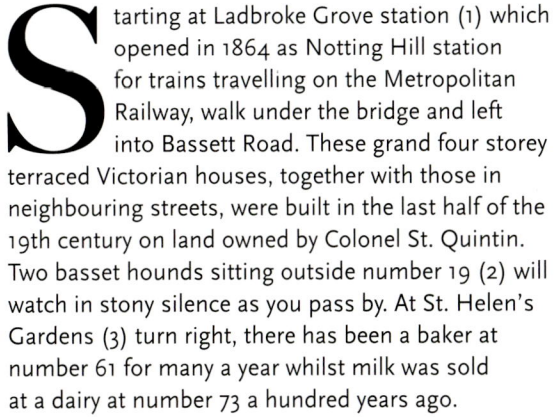

Starting at Ladbroke Grove station (1) which opened in 1864 as Notting Hill station for trains travelling on the Metropolitan Railway, walk under the bridge and left into Bassett Road. These grand four storey terraced Victorian houses, together with those in neighbouring streets, were built in the last half of the 19th century on land owned by Colonel St. Quintin. Two basset hounds sitting outside number 19 (2) will watch in stony silence as you pass by. At St. Helen's Gardens (3) turn right, there has been a baker at number 61 for many a year whilst milk was sold at a dairy at number 73 a hundred years ago.

Bear left in to St. Quintin Avenue and peep through railings into Community Kitchen Gardens (4) where local residents grow fresh produce in raised beds on a former tennis court. Turn right at Pangbourne Avenue, the Princess Louise of

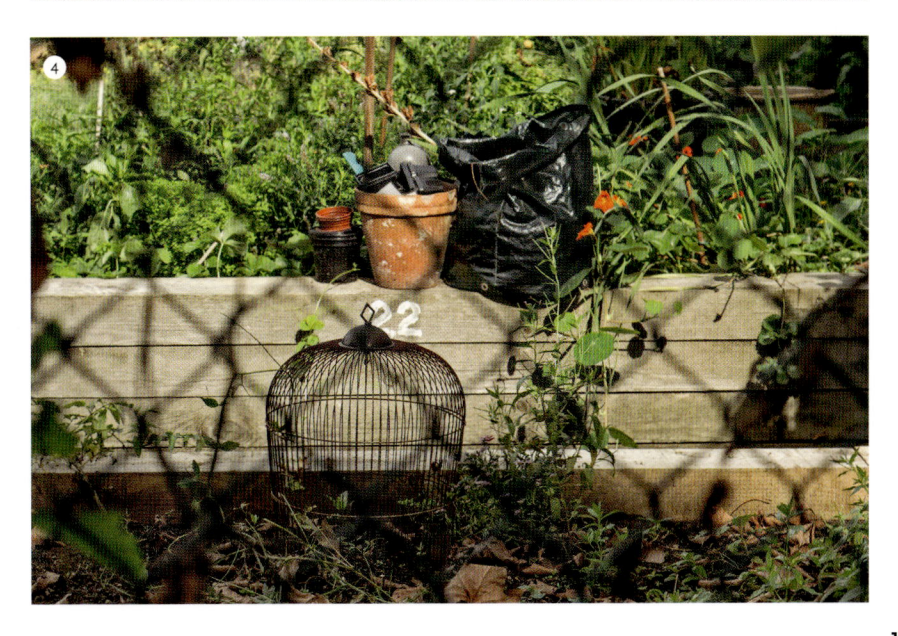

Kensington Nursing Home is a reminder of the former children's hospital established here in 1928 by that Princess. At Barlby Road go right and pause to look up Rootes Drive, the soaring gasometer behind Sunbeam Gardens (5) is a legacy of the former Western Gas Company works built in 1845 overlooking the Paddington Arm of the Grand Union Canal which has now become a nature paradise as it meanders through this part of London.

The imposing 1903 Ladbroke Hall was built by the Earl of Shrewsbury as the main administrative building for his Clement-Talbot automobile factory. During the First World War it became an aero-engine factory, by the 1930s the company was producing the popular Sunbeam cars and was eventually taken over by the Rootes Group. Notting Barn Road (6) running alongside the building is a reminder of the farm which stood nearby and gave its name to the Notting Hill area. When built in 1911, Pall Mall Deposit was the first reinforced depository to be erected in the UK and had space to store thousands of pieces of household furniture and effects.

Turning right into Exmoor Street takes you past the St. Charles Centre. In 1889 the St. Marylebone Infirmary, later renamed St. Charles Hospital (7), moved here to newly built premises and was able to treat more than 700 patients in five pavilions grouped round a central tower whilst local undertaker John Nodes soon established his funeral service in buildings in Hewer Street (8) opposite.

Next to the hospital is one of London's best-kept secrets – the Carmelite Monastery – where a silent order of nuns live a cloistered life, only leaving the grounds for medical purposes. Bear left round the corner of St. Charles Square, continue straight ahead to Ladbroke Grove, cross over and take first left into Telford Road which leads to small Athlone Park. Turn right into Portobello Road and at Faraday Road, one of the several streets around here named after prominent engineers and scientists, is the splendid modern and futuristic looking fire station.

Pause at the junction with Golborne Road (9) for the impressive view to your left of architect Erno Goldfinger's Trellick Tower which when completed in 1972 was the tallest residential building in Europe. Continuing down Portobello, the road follows the curving brick wall of a former Franciscan convent which is now the thriving Spanish school whilst modern housing on the left is built on the site of the old farmhouse belonging to Portobello Farm.

This northern part of Portobello Road is famed for its vintage clothing shops as well as an eclectic mix of shops including Honest Jon's, a 'must' for record lovers of reggae, soul and jazz. At weekends crowds throng to Portobello Green Market (10) which is overlooked by one of Banksy's iconic pieces of street art. Continue under Westway and at the junction with Tavistock Road look up at a blue plaque to Claudia Jones, Mother of the Caribbean Carnival in Britain.

A right turn takes you into Lancaster Road, the Serbian Orthodox Church of St. Sava is housed in the former St. Columb church which was famous for its High Church liturgy whilst in 2010 Chepstow House School found a new home in a former Victorian school. On the corner with Ladbroke Grove stands North Kensington Library which opened its doors to book lovers in 1891, the splendid golden weather vane sitting atop its tower shines brightly on sunny days. It is here the walk ends with Ladbroke Grove station just to your right.

Walk devised by Caroline MacMillan *www.westlondonwalks.co.uk*

Ladbroke Grove

Below left: The Free Library on the corner of Ladbroke Grove and Lancaster Road, as it was known when it opened in 1891, displayed signs 'Silence is Requested'.

Acklam Road

Below: The first Acklam Footbridge crossing the railway opened in 1870.
Page 163: Banksy Mural on Acklam Road

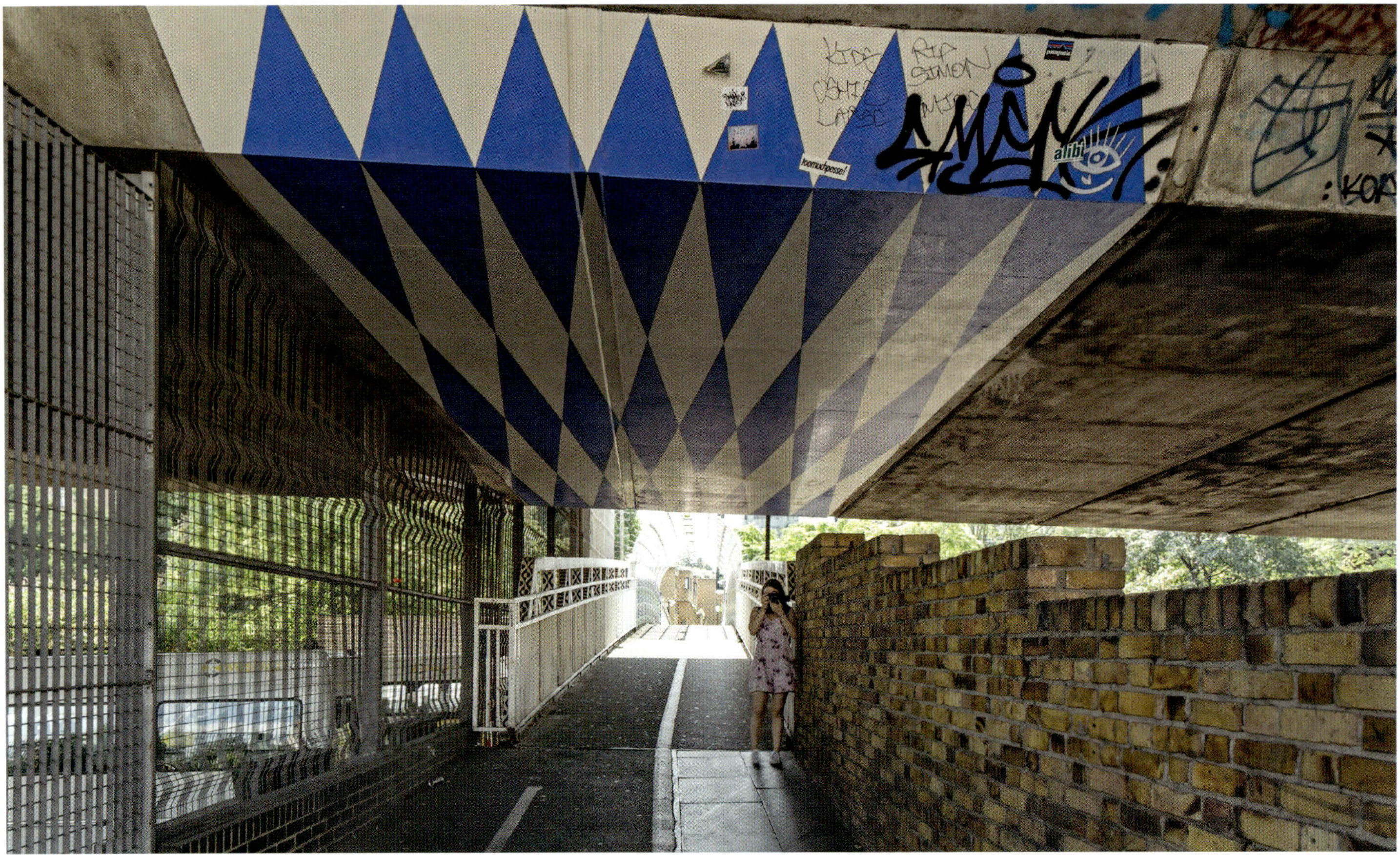

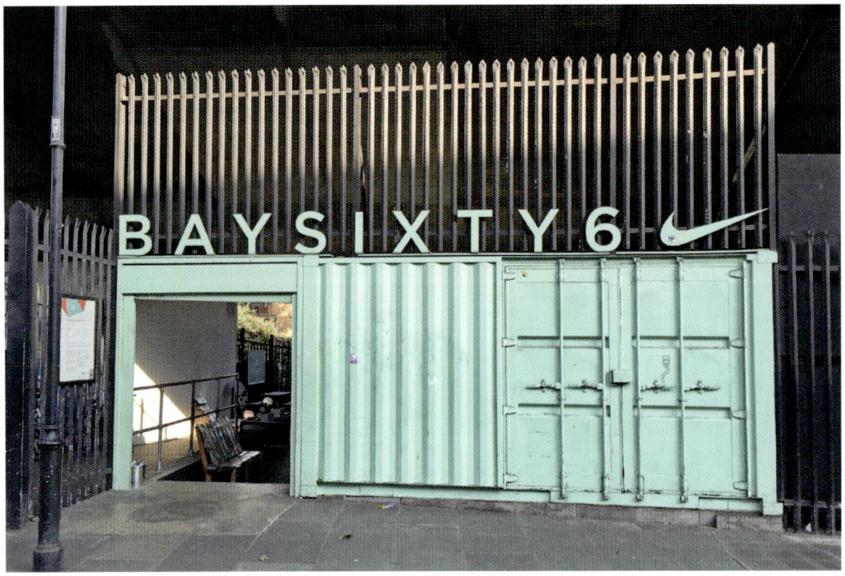
BAYSIXTY6

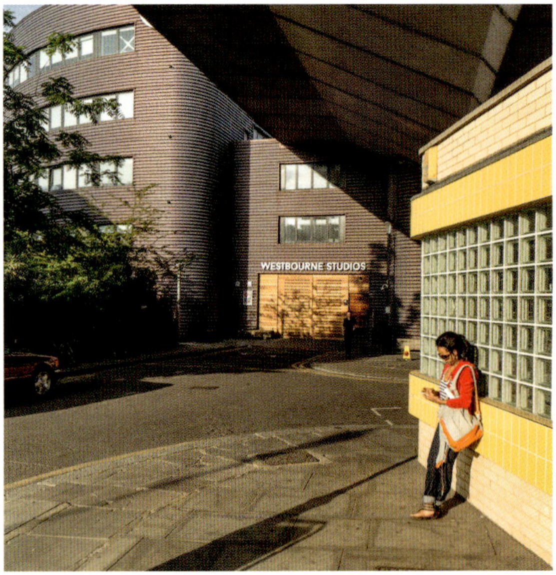
WESTBOURNE STUDIOS

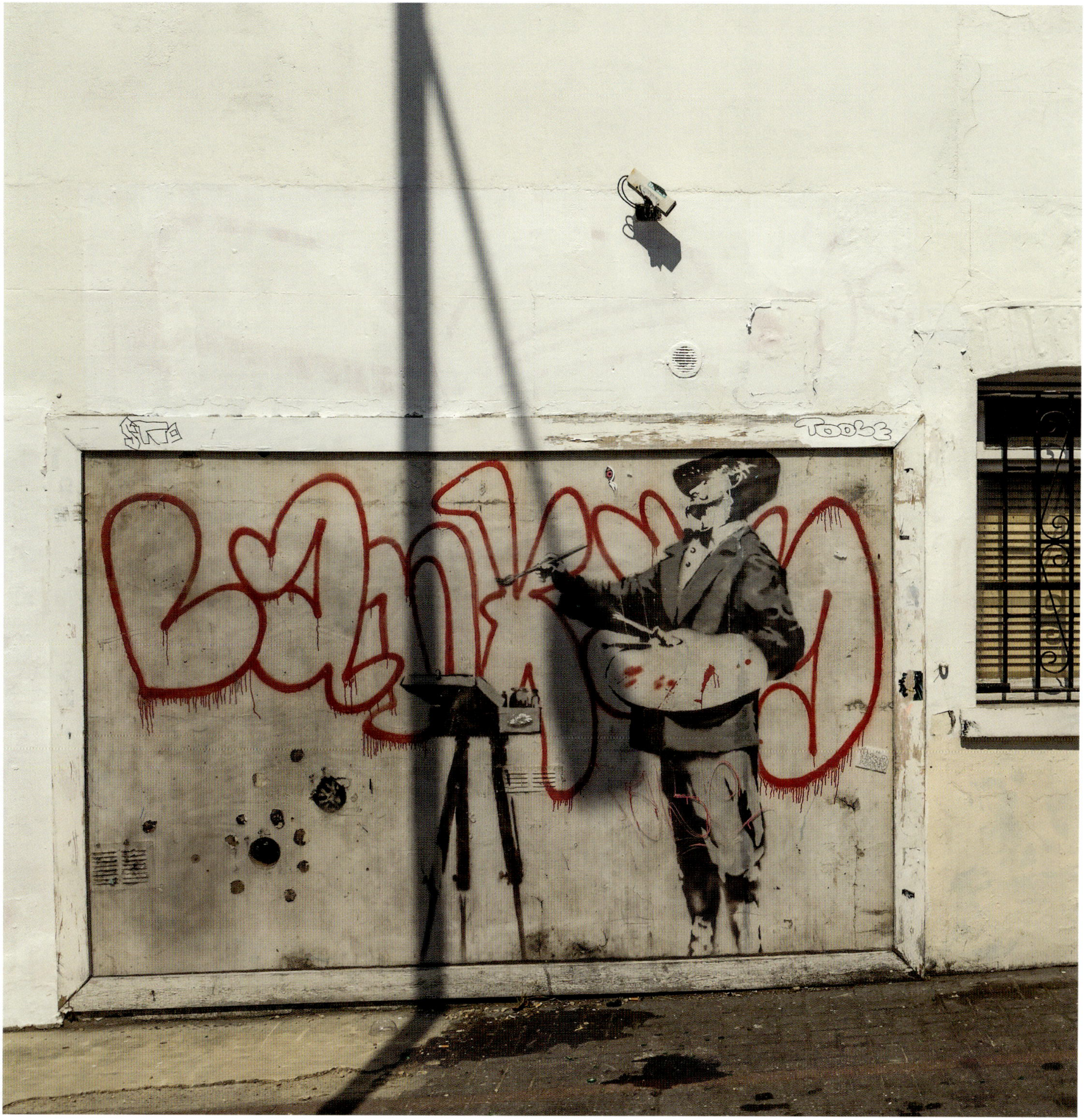

Under the Westway

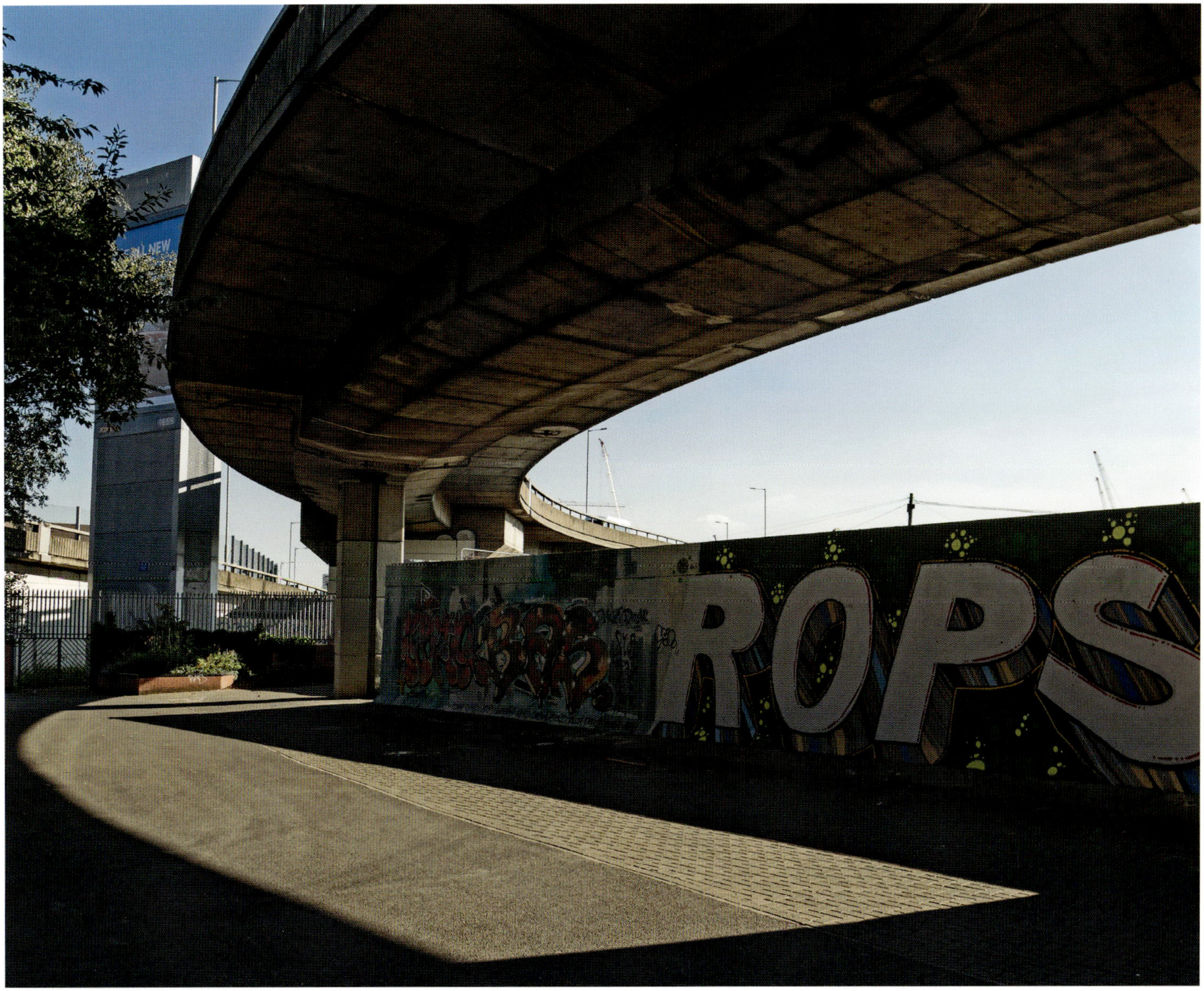
ROPS

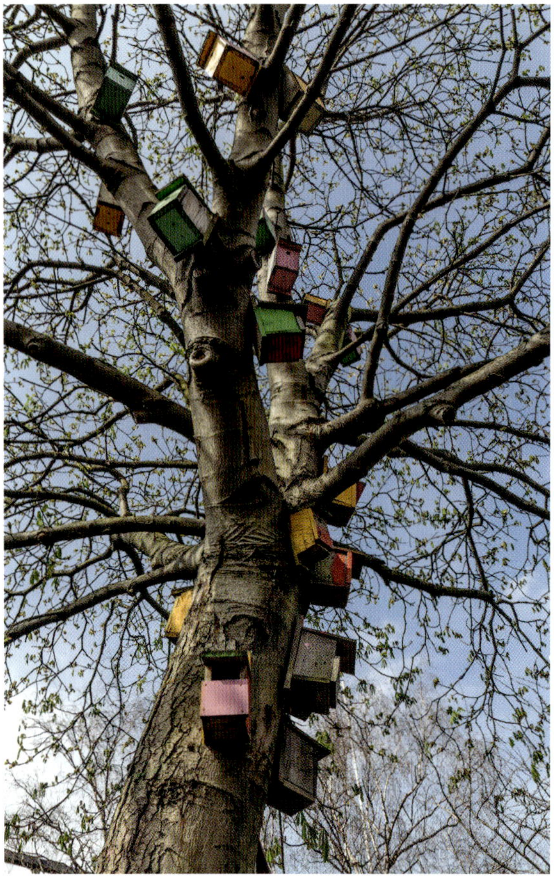

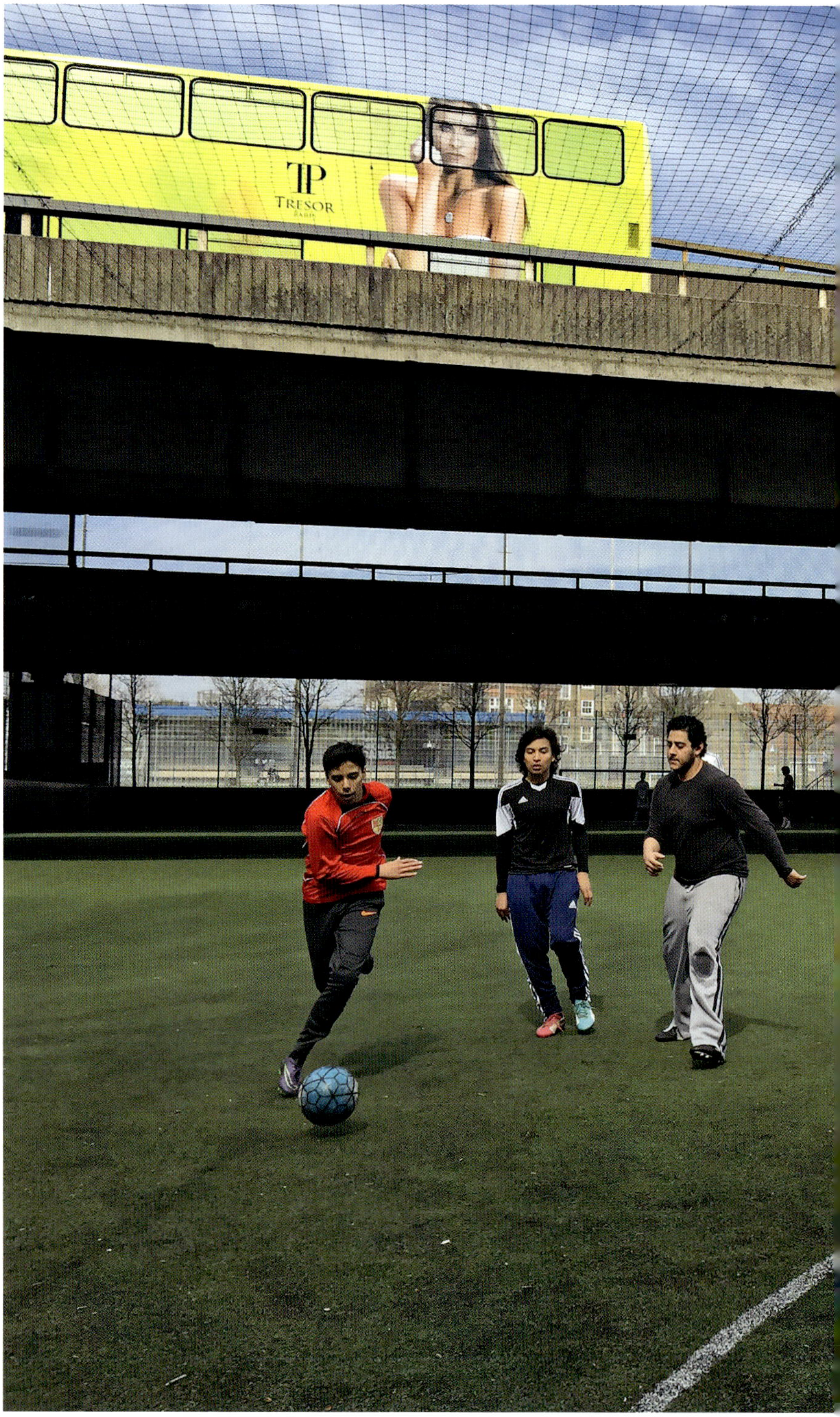
TRESOR

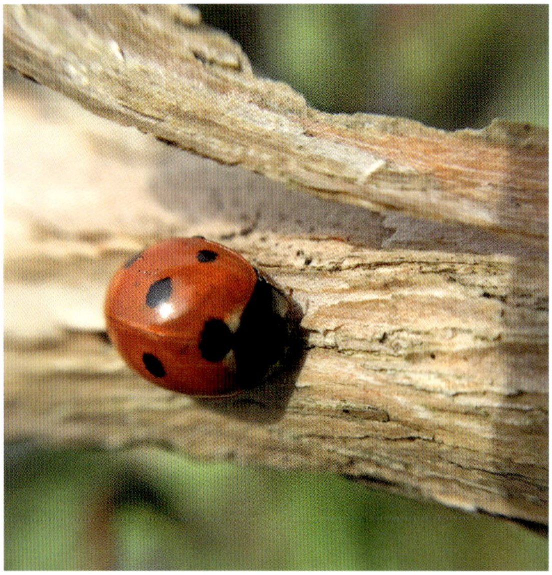

Tucked under the Westway are 23 acres of world-class sports facilities including eight football pitches, ten tennis courts and one of the tallest climbing walls in the UK, which are run by a charitable trust for the benefit of local people.

Overleaf: The striking graffiti found in Crowthorne Road.

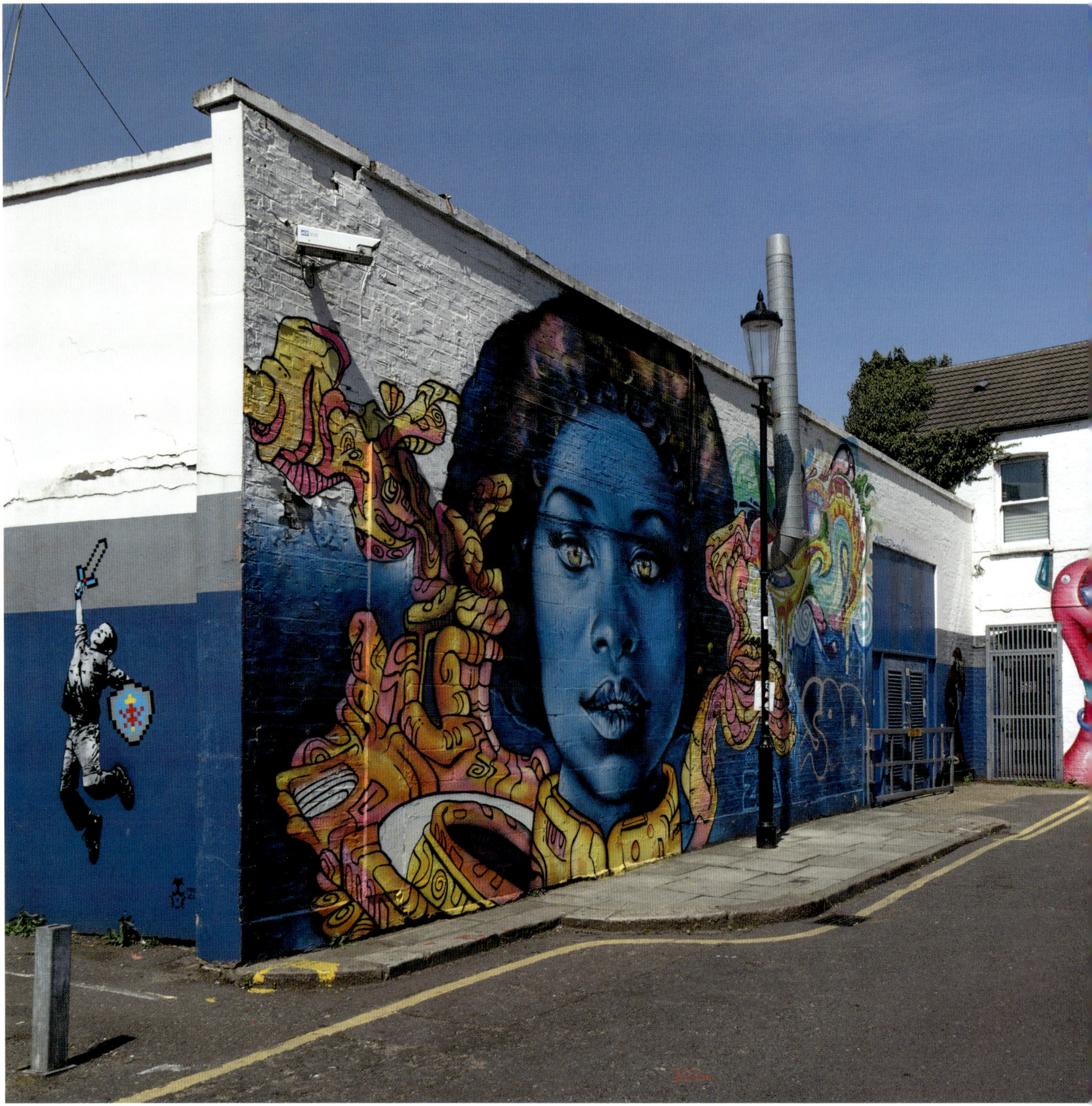

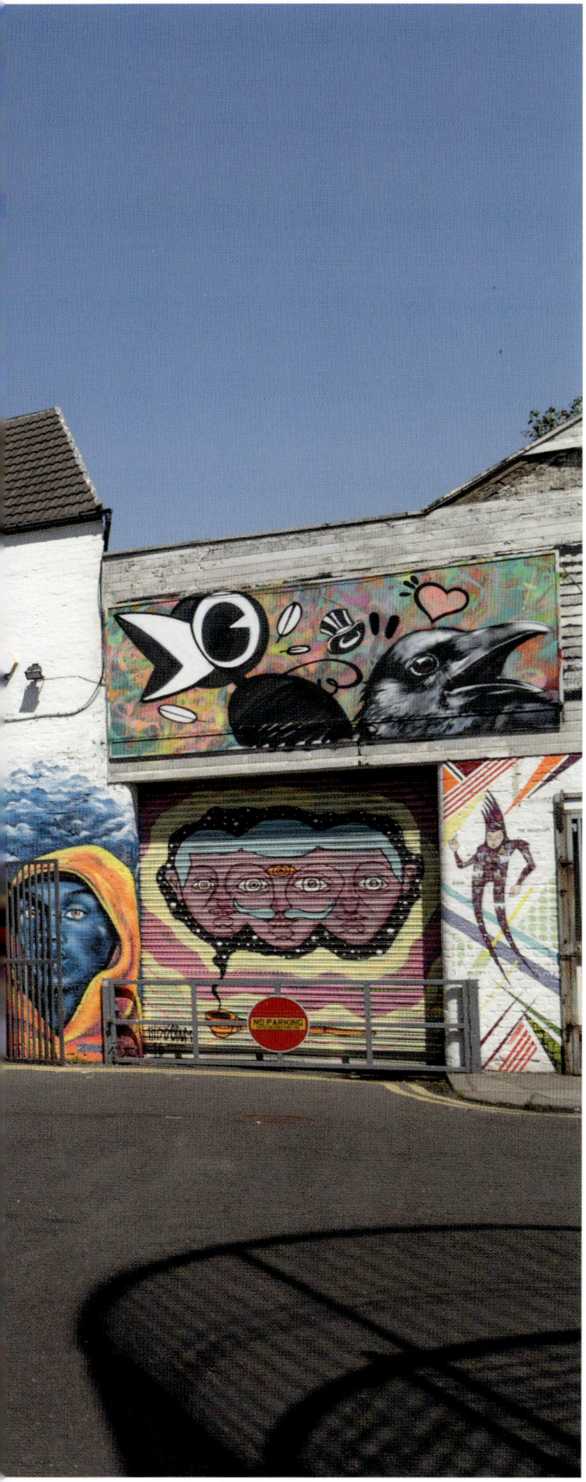
NO PARKING

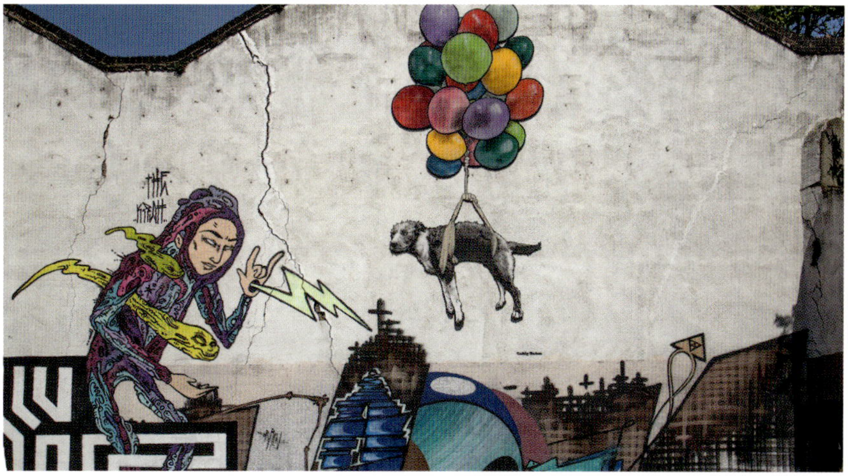

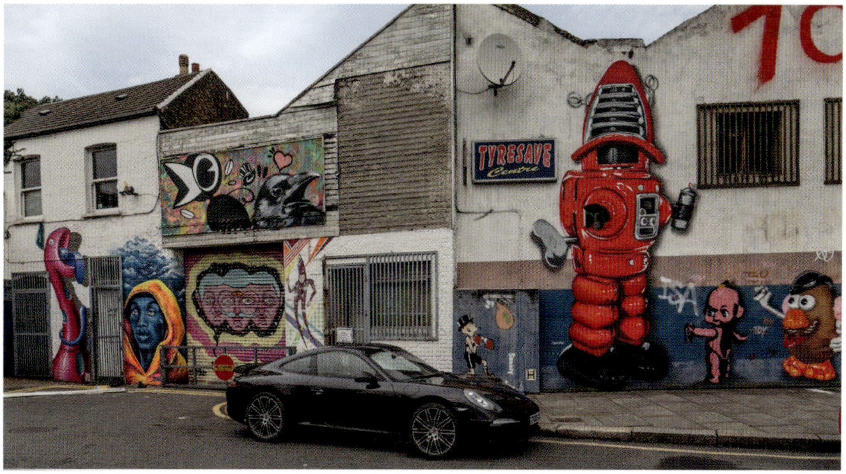
TYRESAVE
Centre

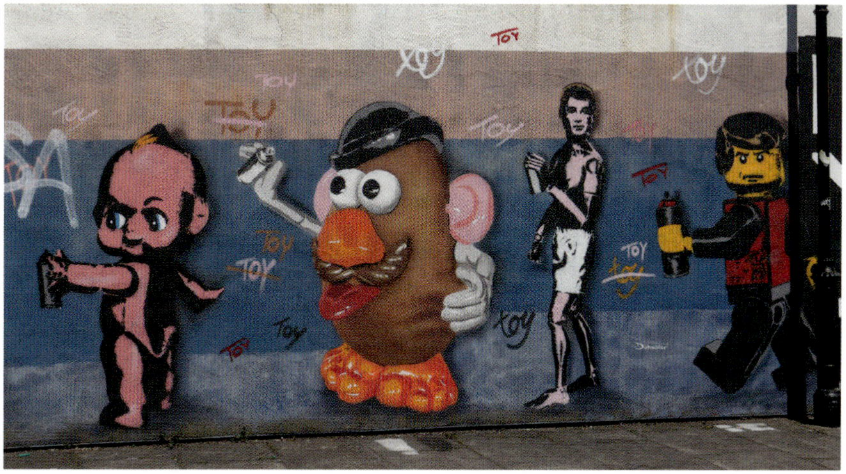
TOY

Kensal Road

This page and opposite top left and right: Opened in 1914 by Emslie John Horniman who donated the land and after whom the garden is named, the Emslie Horniman Pleasance Garden is the traditional starting point for the Notting Hill Carnival. The walled garden in arts and craft style was designed by noted architect Charles Voysey.

Opposite bottom right: Built in 1880, the Cobden Working Men's Club and Institute is named after the 19th century radical politician Richard Cobden and within ten years had a membership of nearly 1,000. It is believed to be the earliest surviving purpose-built working men's club in the country.

171

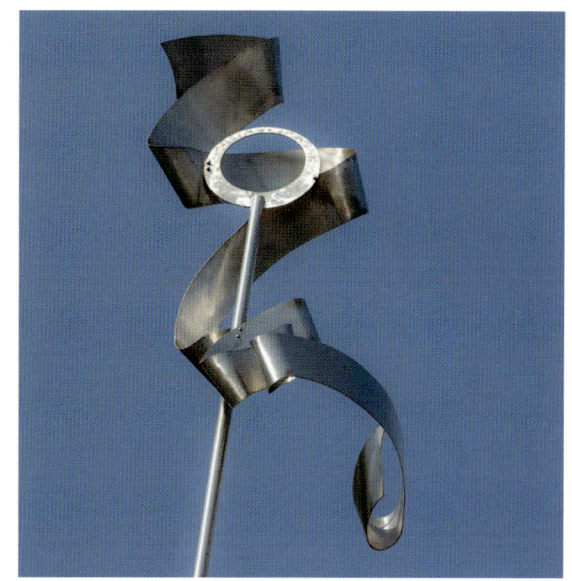

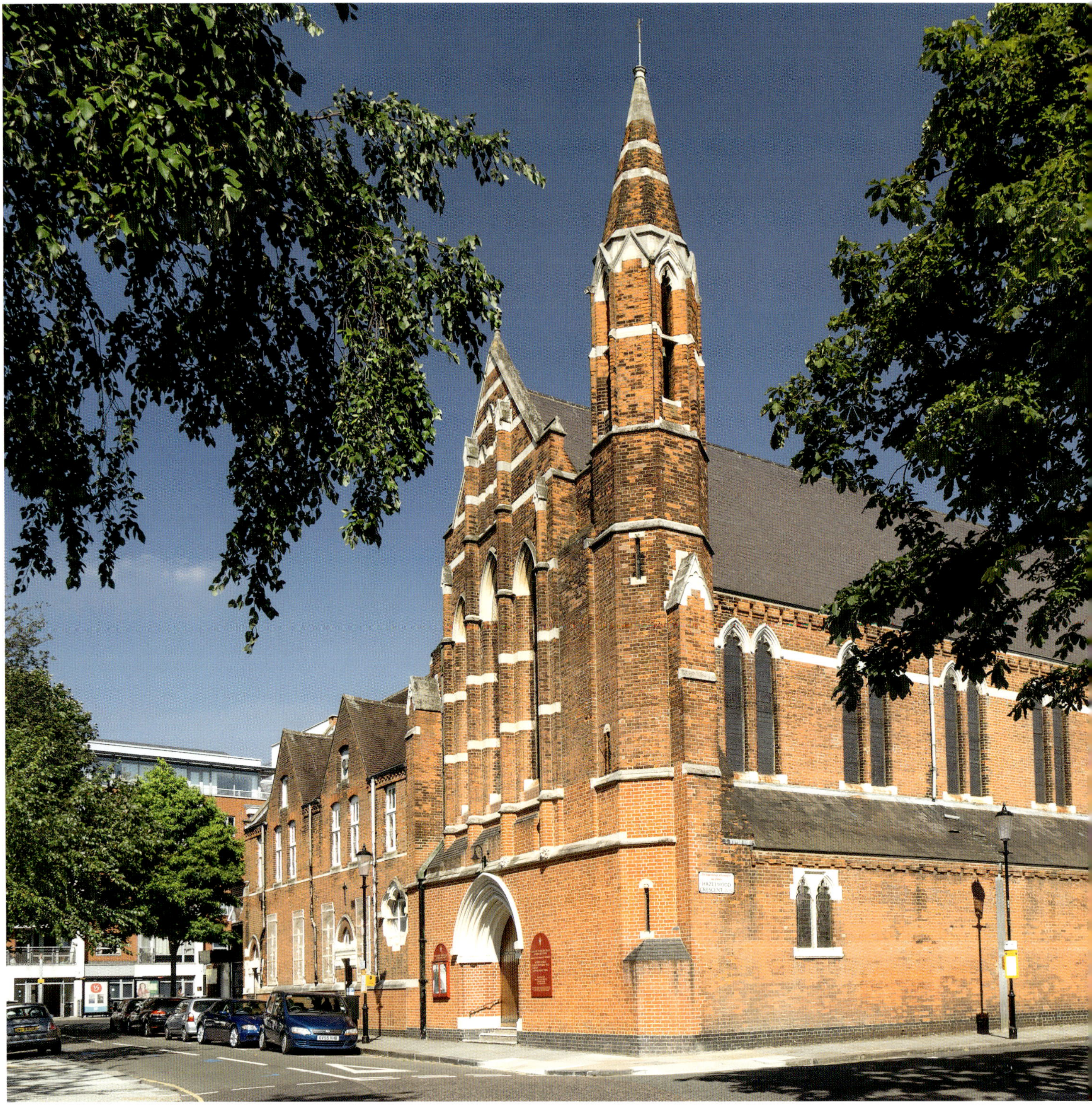

Opposite: The fine lofty brick Roman Catholic Church of Our Lady of the Holy Souls was established by the Oblates of St. Charles, Bayswater and consecrated in 1882.

Right: The former premises of The Globe Wenicke Company who started producing their famous bookcases in 1899, are decorated with fine dragons.

Portobello Road

Right: The view of Portobello Road from the Portobello Terrace Thai Buffet.

Opposite: The restaurant as seen from the street.

By the time Portobello Road has dipped under the Westway and reached North Kensington the antique shops and costermongers selling fruit and vegetables have given way to vintage clothing and second hand goods (picture bottom right and the dangling figure and the car pictures overleaf).

Over the years people from all over of the world have settled in the area and this is reflected in the international flavour of the shops and restaurants.

Top: Junction of Elgin Crescent and Portobello Road at the turn of the last century (left) and today (right).

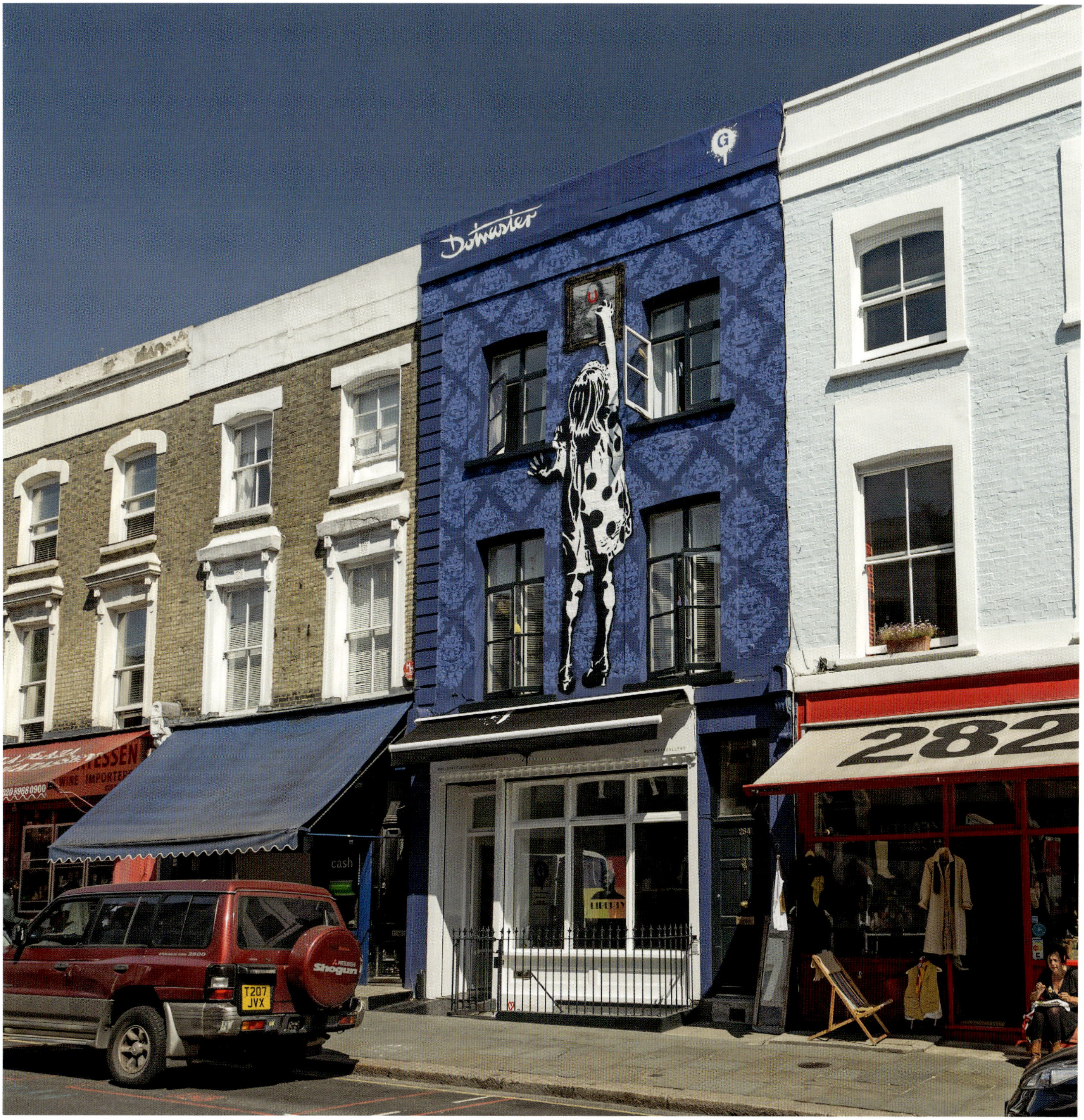

Dotmaster
282
cash
LIBERTY
Shogun
T207
JVX

Bassett Road

Two basset hounds sitting outside number 19 will watch in stony silence as you pass by.

Chesterton Road

The springtime blossom reminds us that a hundred and fifty years ago this area was the Notting Barns farmland owned by Colonel St. Quintin who instigated the building of the handsome streets we see today.

Opposite top and bottom right: Strange thin building in Norburn Street, off Chesterton Road.

181

Oxford and Cambridge Gardens

Cambridge Gardens is said to be haunted by a ghostly No. 7 bus. The tale is that a young motorist was killed at the junction with St. Mark's Road in the 1930s when his car swerved off the road for no apparent reason and hit a lamp post. Witnesses since have claimed to see a London Transport bus tearing down the road towards them and swinging their vehicles off the road to avoid it, then looking back where there is no bus to be seen. The No. 7 bus still takes this same route down Cambridge Gardens.

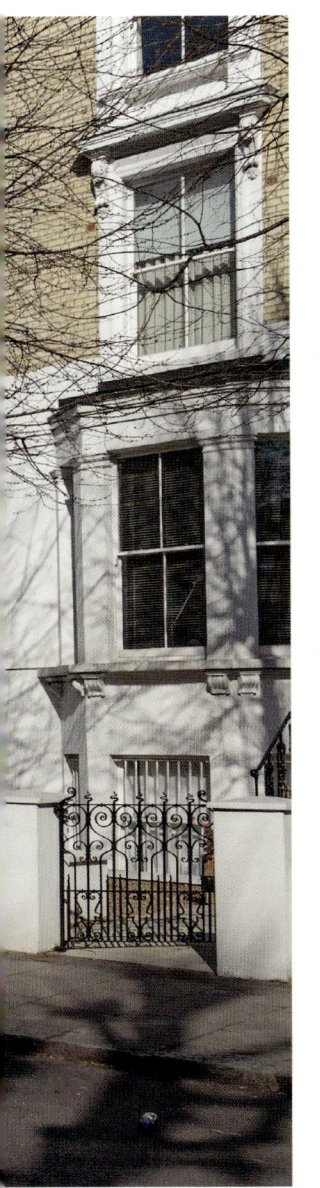

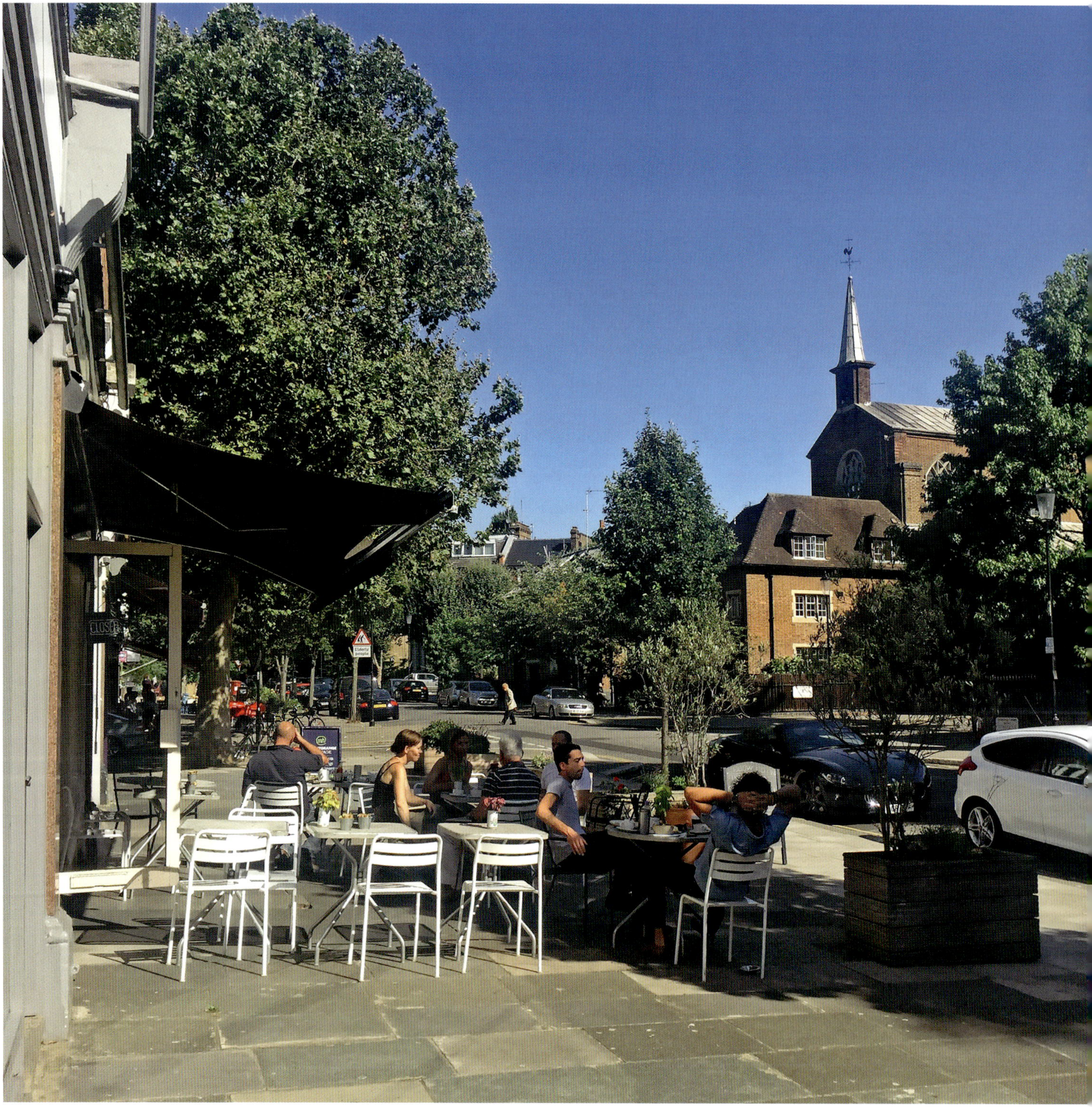

St. Helen's Gardens is a favourite place for local residents to enjoy a coffee and watch the world go by.

Kensington Memorial Park

Opened in 1926 by Princess Louise, Duchess of Argyll, the park was a tribute to those who had given their lives in the First World War.

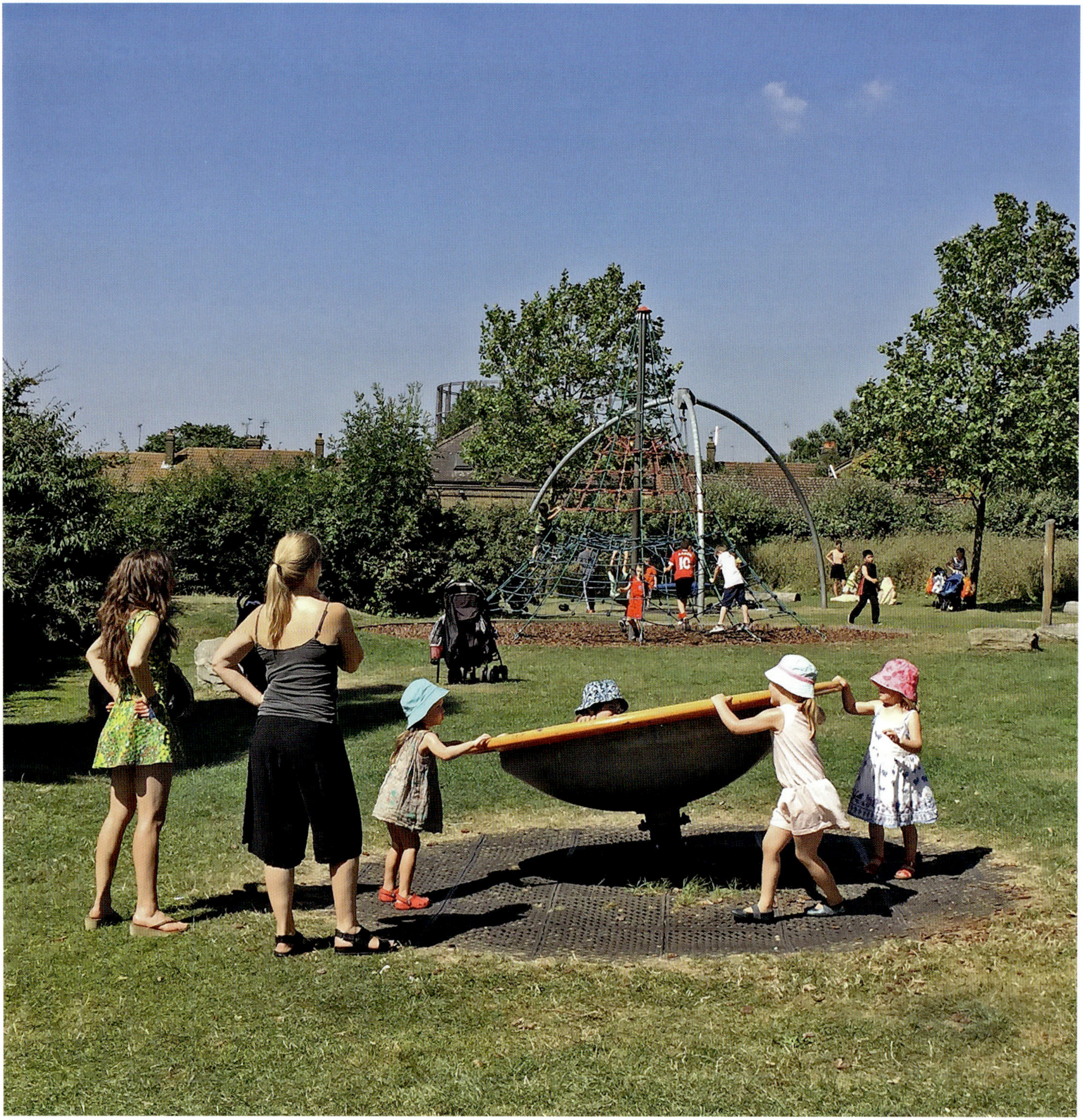

The innovative playground and water play area is a firm favourite for families with young children, particularly on hot summer days.

Trellick Tower

Designed in brutalist style in 1972 by architect Erno Goldfinger (who fell out with author Ian Fleming and so is immortalised as the baddie in the James Bond stories), Trellick Tower is a towering landmark just north of the Westway in North Kensington. Whilst some flats remain under council management, many are now owned privately. Love it or hate it, as it is a Grade II* listed building looks like being here to stay.

Left top and bottom: The approach to the railway bridge at the top of Golborne Road is decorated in a mass of handmade tiles, all personalised.

Golborne Road

Until the middle of the 19th century Golborne Road was no more than a country footpath crossing the fields of Portobello Farm. But with the widening of the road in 1870 shops were built and the road was extended over the railway. Once a notorious slum area, today it is a magnet for shops, galleries and restaurants catering for the well-to-do residents who have moved here in recent years. Different communities have shaped the neighbourhood's character and this is reflected in the diversity of food stores including Portuguese patisseries and Moroccan cafés.

150
PET SHOP

SNAPS + RYE
WE ARE
TIME OUT
LONDON'S
TOP 50
AKVAVIT
COCKTAILS
SKÅL!

195

Grand Union Canal

The Paddington Arm of the Grand Union Canal is one of London's secret highways. The waterway drifts slowly by old factories and modern supermarkets, whilst the large landmark gas holder can be seen for miles around.

When the canal opened, the Paddington Canal Company placed a footbridge where no road existed and charged a halfpenny toll, gaining it the nickname 'Halfpenny Steps'. It was later replaced by the Wedlake Street bridge (inset opposite and from where the main pictures overleaf were taken from).

Narrow boats often transported coffins to Kensal Rise Cemetery where they were received at specially built landing platforms.

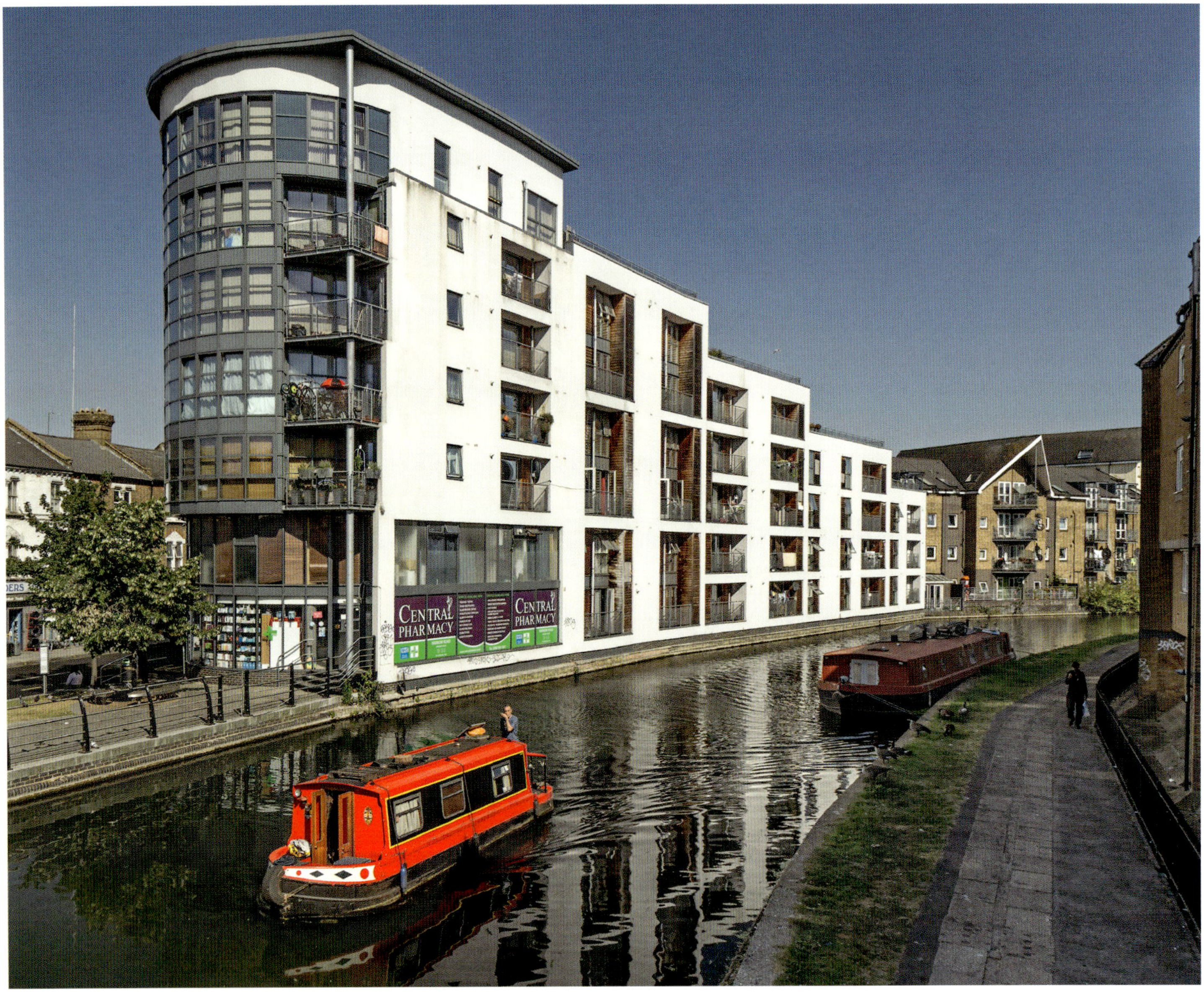
CENTRAL PHARMACY
CENTRAL PHARMACY

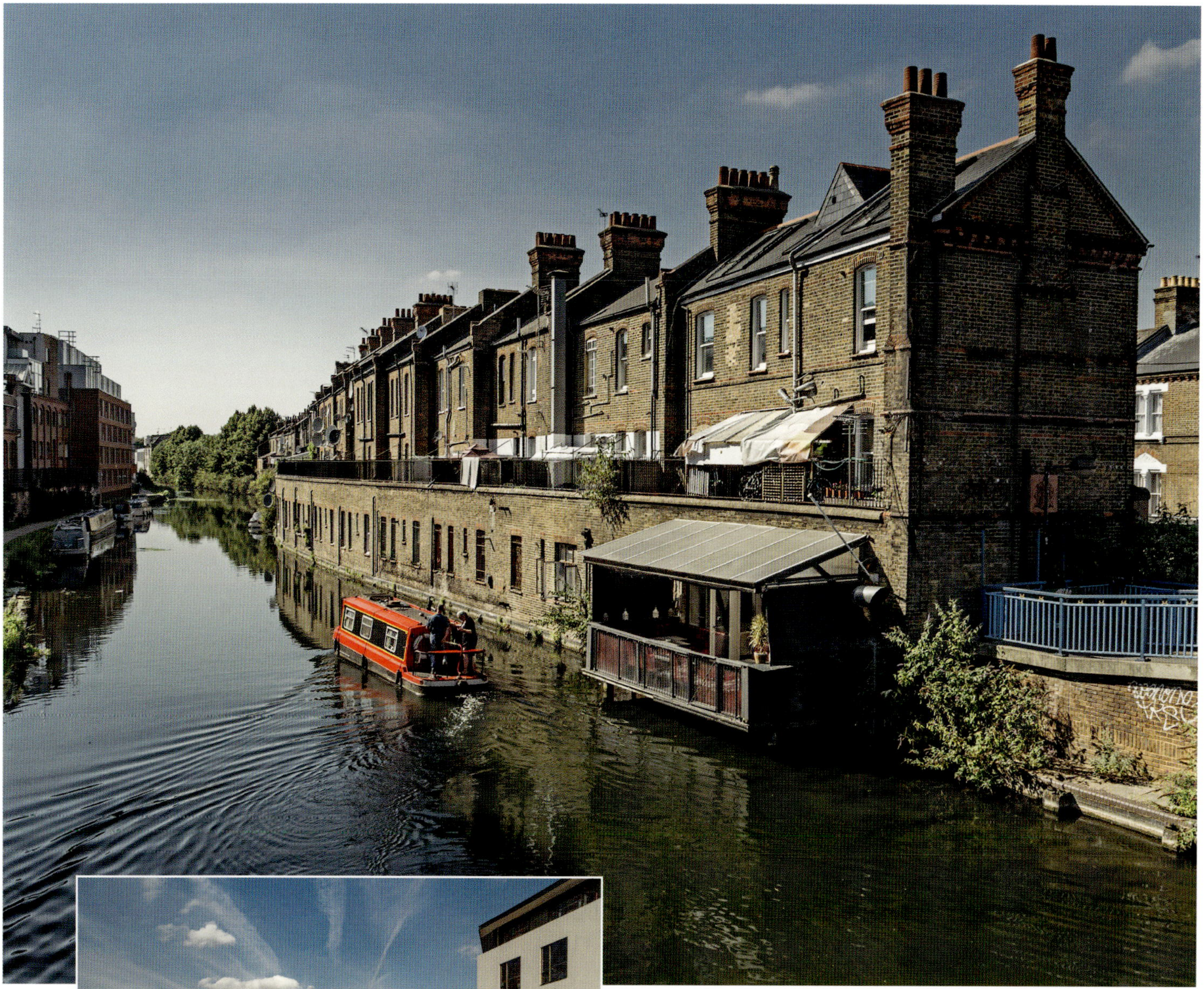

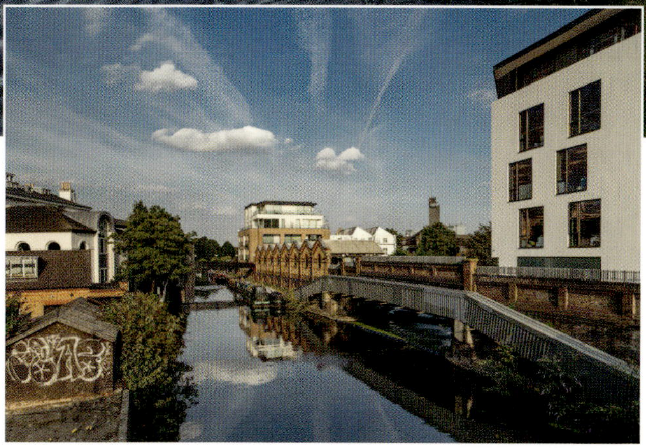

200

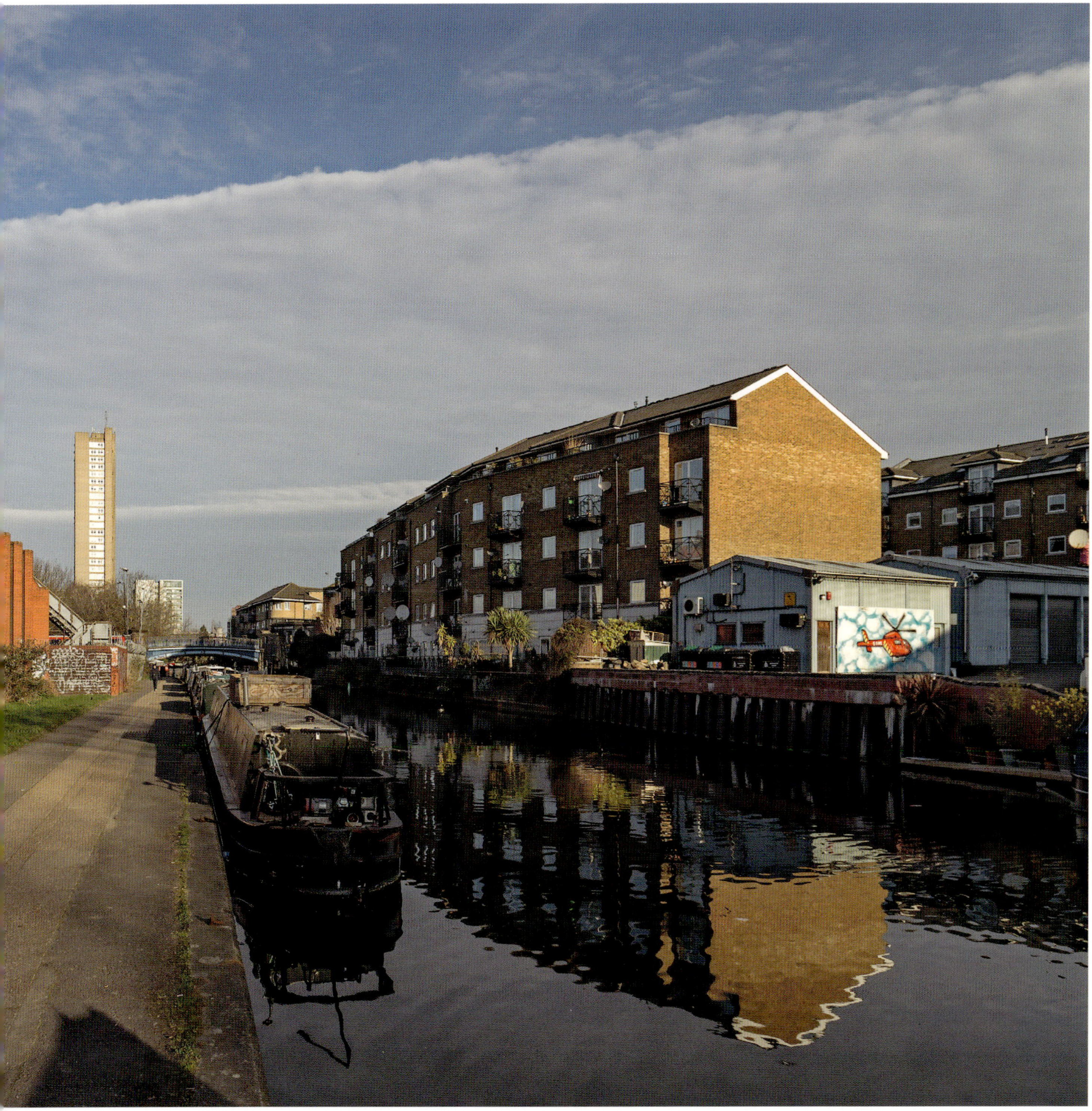

Meanwhile Gardens with its wildlife garden is a well loved green sanctuary and gives joy to the local community of this northern part of Kensington.

203

Thank you to all the staff at Winkworth Notting Hill and North Kensington offices for their kind support of this book.

NOTTING HILL

178 Westbourne Grove
Notting Hill, London W11 2RH

020 7727 3227

nottinghill@winkworth.co.uk
www.winkworth.co.uk

NORTH KENSINGTON

141 Ladbroke Grove
North Kensington, London W10 6HJ

020 7792 5000

northkensington@winkworth.co.uk
www.winkworth.co.uk

Winkworth

All rights reserved. No part of this publication may be reproduced, stored in any retrieval system or transmitted in any form or by any means, electronic, mechanical photocopying or otherwise without the prior permission of the copyright holders. Whilst every care has been taken in the production of this book, no responsibility can be accepted for any errors or omissions. The publishers have taken all reasonable care in compiling this work but cannot accept responsibility for the information derived from third parties, which has been reproduced in good faith.

First Edition – ©Unity Print and Publishing Limited 2016

History Consultant:
Caroline MacMillan
www.westlondonwalks.co.uk

Editorial Assistant: Amy Wilson
(pictured above in Portobello Road)

Designed by Ball Design & Branding
www.balldesignconsultancy.com

Printed by Page Brothers of Norwich
www.pagebros.co.uk

Bound by Green Street Bindery of Oxford. www.maltbysbookbinders.com

Colour Management by
Paul Sherfield of The Missing Horse Consultancy
www.missinghorsecons.co.uk

Published by Unity Print and Publishing Limited,
18 Dungarvan Avenue,
London SW15 5QU

Tel: +44 (0)20 8487 2199
aw@unity-publishing.co.uk
www.unity-publishing.co.uk

Follow Andrew on Twitter: @andrewpics

Turvens Lane

Farm
Turvens House

Shepherds Bush

Turvens Lane

Mr Greens Greens